# THE
# VEGETARIAN TASTE
# OF THAILAND

First published 1997 by

**SLG BOOKS**
**PO Box 9465**
**Berkeley,CA 94709**
**Tel: 510-525-1134**
**Fax: 510-525-2632**

**Editor: Roger Williams**
**Introduction by John Bear**
**Foreword by Roger Williams & Yuk Wah Lee**
**Photographs by Mr. Suksan Samranrit**

**Cover design by Prayut Sangvishean**
**Book design by Prayut Sangvishean**
**Cover rendering by Linel Aujnoti**
**Color separations and printing by**
**Snow Lion Graphics**
**Berkeley/Hong Kong**

**Library of Congress Cataloging-in-Publication Data**

Pinyo Srisawat, 1956-
    The vegetarian taste of Thailand : vegetable, tofu, and seafood
dishes / by Pinyo Srisawat & Yingsak Jonglertjesdawong.
        p.  cm.
    Includes index
    ISBN 0-943389-14-3. -- ISBN 0-943389-13-5
    1. Vegetarian cookery. 2. Cookery, Thai. 3. Cookery--Thailand-
    -Cha-am. 4. Cookery (Seafood)   I.Yingsak Jonglertjesdawong, 1956-
        II. Title.
    TX837.P55 1996                          96-42142
    641.5'636--DC20                         CIP

# THE VEGETARIAN TASTE OF THAILAND

## VEGETABLE, TOFU & SEAFOOD DISHES
### FROM CHA AM RESTAURANTS

PINYO SRISAWAT
&
YINGSAK JONGLERTJESDAWONG

SLG BOOKS
BERKELEY/HONG KONG

# FOREWORD

**W**hen Pinyo, a.k.a. Jimmy, Srisawat first approached us to publish a Thai cookbook based on recipes from his very popular Thai restaurant Cha Am in Berkeley I had my reservations. Reservations, that is, aside from the almost weekly ones my partner and I had at his Cha Am restaurant which just happened to be around the corner from our office in north Berkeley.

Three years, many recipe-testing meals and a lot of work later SLG Books published "**The Elegant Taste of Thailand**": Cha Am Cuisine. With virtually no advertising and a scattering of very good reviews the first printing sold out in less than ten months. Its easy-to-use recipes and superb color photographs made Thai cooking accessible to Western cooks of all levels. While we were extremely pleased with our book's popularity in America we were ecstatic when it became a best seller in Thailand and a respected textbook in Thai cooking schools in Bangkok. Its availability in the Bangkok airport, Asia Books' bookstores and many of the better hotels in Thailand certainly helped. We will soon be going to press with our eighth printing of "**The Elegant Taste of Thailand**".

Over the years many fans of "**The Elegant Taste of Thailand**" have repeatedly requested that we do a Thai cookbook with more vegetarian dishes; lighter but still distinctly Thai dishes that appeal to the more health conscious among devoted Thai food fans.

With those goals in mind Jimmy approached his old friend Yingsak Jonglertjesdawong of the Institute of Culinary Art in Bangkok. Three years, many recipe testing meals and a lot of work later we are proud to present to you "**The Vegetarian Taste of Thailand: Vegetable, Tofu, and Seafood Dishes**".

It is our supreme desire that "**The Vegetarian Taste of Thailand**" with its creative uses of gluten, vegetables, tofu and seafood will satiate the palates of our most discerning health conscious gourmets. We are certain that the spectacular photographs of the beautifully presented dishes herein will titillate your appetite.

Good Luck and Good Eating

Roger Williams & Yuk Wah Lee
Berkeley, California, July 4, 1996

# CONTENTS

# INTRODUCTION

**I**t seems almost inconceivable to me that it is less than twenty years since Thai cooking arrived(1) on the shores of America,(2) in my own consciousness and, significantly,(3) on my taste buds. I am embarrassed to think that in the 1970's I might well have said, sitting on some chrome-and-naugahyde chair eating sweet and sour pork or sukiyaki, "Ah, yes, I am indeed a connoisseur of Asian cookery. Pass the chow mein and the triple-fried egg rolls, please." How little I knew of what was in store.

Enjoying great food and being unaware of Thai cuisine is rather like getting to Agra and somehow missing the Taj Mahal, or spending all your time in the Bolivian hat room at the Louvre and not getting around to the Mona Lisa.

And suddenly, almost overnight it seemed, we were up to our elbows in Pad Thai. In Berkeley, where I lived in the 80's, Thai restaurants were popping up faster than the wildflowers in the spring. Often they were the main topic of conversation, as those whose quest for great food experiences communicated back and forth. "Have you tried Restaurant A?" "Yes, but it was not as good as B." "We had a fine Ped Yang at C, but the duck was a little soggy." "Try it at D, it was nice and crisp." And on and on and on.

Some of the restaurants were good, some were very good, and a few bordered on greatness. But it was not until the arrival in Berkeley, in 1985, of Pinyo Srisawat and his Cha Am restaurant, that we truly appreciated the heights to which Thai cuisine could rise.
We had not only come upon the Taj Mahal, but on the night of the full moon, with the string quartet softly playing Bach in the background.

Many superb meals were enjoyed at Cha Am, and with the arrival of **The Elegant Taste of Thailand** in 1989, my wife and I were actually emboldened to try to prepare some of the dishes ourselves. The fact that by this time we were living 3,000 miles from Berkeley, well out side Cha Am's delivery zone, was an added impetus to try one of our favorites, Kai Yang (Thai style barbecued chicken) ourselves. It was a huge success, and there are many important stains on the pages of **The Elegant Taste of Thailand** to attest to our subsequent efforts.

And yet, like so many in the health-conscious 90's, we found ourselves doing less and less cooking with rich sauces, red meats, and all those other items promoted by the Cholesterol Council. If only, we thought on more than on occasion, the glorious Thai cooking of Cha Am, as recorded in **The Elegant Taste of Thailand,** could be transformed overnight into a health-conscious, vegetarian (all right, some fish dishes as well, please) cuisine.

Well it wasn't overnight, but, thankfully, it *did* happen, and the result is that which you hold in your hands. The co-authors are just right for this task. One is the chef-owner of the Cha Am restaurants, familiar with western tastes and wishes and the availabilities in the food world; the other owns his own culinary institute in Thailand where he has a popular television cooking program, and offers the vast experience of bringing classic and innovative Thai cuisine into the health-conscious world.

When I looked at an early version of this book, I had two thoughts and one worry.

Thought 1 was that it was exactly what I had been hoping for.

Thought 2 was that the food photos were, if anything, even more impressive than those in the first book in the series. I believe I gained four pounds just looking at them.

And the worry was that somehow it might be too complicated for the likes of me. Would I be able to find some of the exotic ingredients? Could I follow the recipes? And, most significantly, would the end product be something worthy of the **Cha Am** name and legend, or just another pedestrian product such that I might as well defrost a Betty Krachathipok Boil-in-a-Bag Thai Dinner?

I need not have worried. (Well, actually I didn't worry too much, but I am a slightly nervous cook at times.) As it happened, I was the "designated dip" at a potluck party a few days after I got my hands on this book, and so it seemed appropriate to try the spicy prawn dip with vegetables. It was fast. It was simple. It was wonderful. It was popular. And, unexpectedly, it was very, very Thai.

I need to explain that "unexpectedly." Why was I surprised when the end product of a Thai recipe in a Thai cookbook truly tasted Thai to me, and was very good Thai at that? What is it that makes something taste Thai? I don't think the English language is capable of capturing the difference among food tastes. Try, for instance, to explain in 10,000 words or less, the difference between a peach and a pear. But one bite and you know.

And so it is with Thai food in general, great Thai food in particular, and the recipes in this book in very, very particular. How is Thai cooking (and especially Cha Am cooking) different from anything Chinese or Cambodian or Japanese or anything else Oriental? Is it the interaction of the lime juice and the chilli sauce? Is there magic in the palm sugar or the tamarind juice? What is the secret chemistry of coconut milk and shallots? Let some scholar write her Master's thesis on these matters: I am content that my palate (and my diner guests) know how very special and how very Thai it all is - even though almost all the ingredients came from my local supermarket.

So sit back and enjoy the magnificent photos of the food and its country of origin. Then start thinking about what you're going to try first, and next, and who you are going to invite to share in the wonderful fruits (and seafood) of your labors, that will surely accrue.

And dream about your first (or your next) trip to the **Cha Am** restaurants of Berkeley and San Francisco, the blessed source of the worthy inspirations for **The Vegetarian Taste of Thailand.**

**John Bear**
**El Cerrito, California February, 1996**

# VEGETARIAN FOOD: SIMPLY THE BEST

## Ignorance or Consciousness

When "ignorance" was born, even though its eyes were closed it was suckled on milk for the first time. As its eyes slowly began to open, the baby learned how to feed itself for survival. Time passed, and the child grew into an adult, developing a fascination with the taste of food, thus "ignorance" learned to eat for satifaction.

But it still did not understand that eating is more than just selecting the menu, ordering food, putting it in your mouth, chewing and swallowing.

Should we worry about such thing? Yes, things have changed, our eyes are wide open now. People do not have to struggle for survival anymore, but still only a few know how to live intelligently.

In modern society, smart people know how to use diet to maintain a healthy and happy life, thus increasing their consciousness while eating. Do not let ignorance rule your life: it's not too late to turn on your awareness.

### Back To Nature

When the invitable question arises of what constitues healthy eating , there seem to be almost as many responses as there are people responding. Nutritionists usually argue that you should eat a little of everything and not too much of anything; scientists, on the other hand, recommend eating certain types of food; whole foods.

The various theories may be confusing, but they can be easily summarized: the best thing for the human body is a vegetarian diet of natural foods. This assertion is no longer considered extraordinary. Two crucial pieces of scientific evidence point to the irrefutable fact that our ancestors were vegetarians.

According to several studies, the abundant foods in ancient times were fruits, vegetables and nuts. During the last Ice Age, however, natural foods were scarce, so human beings turned to eating animal flesh, continuing this habit to the present day either by necessity or by habit. Some groups of people have remained primarily vegetarians, such as the Hunzakuts, an ethnic tribe in northern Pakistan whose members are known for living long healthy lives.

**Moreover,** during times of crisis brought on by war, such as the Allied blockade of Germany and Denmark in 1917-1918, or the food shortage in Norway during the First World War, when people were forced to live on a diet of grains, vegetables, fruits and dairy products, their health improved immensely.

The second piece of supporting evidence has to do with our anatomy. It is a little known fact that human physiology is completely different from that of other carnivorous animals. Human characteristics are indentical to fruit eaters and very similar to grass eaters, but not at all like meat eaters. Human natural instincts are also basically non-carnivorous.

**Physiologically, anatomically and instinctively, human beings are perfectly suited to a diet of fruits, vegetables, nuts and grains.**

### Healthy Eating, Smart Living

"A full belly is the mother of Evil."

-Poor Richard's Almanac

You are what you eat, because health is very closely linked to nutrition. Historically, vegetarianism has been praticed from the time of the early Greeks for various reasons, coinciding with a belief in the transmigration of souls. In the Sixth Century B.C., the Greek philosopher **Pythagoras** was a prominent vegetarian, urging abstention from meat; **Empedocles** followed his lead in the Fifth Century B.C.

By the Eighteenth Century, the rationale for refraining from meat had acquired economic and ethical as well as nutritional dimensions. Noteworthy vegetarians included **Benjamin Franklin** and **Voltaire**. Franklin was the first remarkable American vegetarian, inspired to try a meatless diet by Thomas Tryoy's writing, *The Way to Health and Long Life & Happiness.*

Since then, influential people have continued to be interested in vegetarianism, such as Horace Greeley, founder of the *New York Herald Tribune.* **"Other things being equal,"** Greeley once said, **"I judge that a strict vegetarian will live ten years longer than a habitual flesh-eater, while suffering on average , less than half as much from sickness as the carnivorous must."**

These ideas are in full accordance with modern medical science. Food intake affects not only health, but personality and behavior. The habit of eating the right foods is easy to acquire and saves trouble in the long term, but wrong dietary habits cause illness; the so-called **"diseases of civilization"**: obesity, cancer, diabetes, heart disease, gout, high blood pressure, bronchitis, gallstones and varicose veins.

Obesity is considered to be a real problem in the Western world; fat people have higher accident rates and tend to die younger. Vegetarians, because of the kinds of food that they eat, are less likely to be fat than meat eaters.

All of these details support the inevitable conclusion that vegetarianism is the right method for healthy living.

### Some Notable Vegetarians

Plato, Socrates, Ovid, Seneca, Clement of Alexandria, Plutarch, Pythagoras, Leonardo da Vinci, Alexander Pope, Sir Issac Newton, Jean Jacques Rousseau, Voltaire, John Milton, Charles Darwin, Percy Bysshe Shelley, Henry David Thoreau, Richard Wagner, Benjamin Franklin, Leo Tolstoy, Mahatma Gandhi, George Bernard Shaw, Albert Schweitzer, and Albert Einstein.

### Enlivening Philosophy

Many kinds of food provide the energy and essential nutrients that a body needs to function properly. Different foods vary in their energy content, measured in calories. Regardless of what kind of food is ingested, as long as the energy input in terms of calories and the energy output in terms of activity are balanced, the body weight will remain constant.

A well-balanced diet is crucial for the maintenance of good health. For that reason, vegetarian diets are strongly recommended. Vegetarian diets are composed mostly of fruits and vegetables, which are highly nutritious and universally recognized as sources of vitamins, minerals and other essential nutrients. Less than one tenth of the calories and 1% of the fat in the food supply come from fruits and vegetables.

Admittedly, there is no such thing as a perfect diet. Some kinds of food may be rich in a certain nutrient but poor in others, but they can be complementary. At this point, it is important to take the two **Q** factors into consideration:

. **quality** - the nutrient composition

. **quantity** - the amount of food taken in

*A vegetarian diet can provide all the nutrients necessary for the body, such as:*

### 1. Proteins

The body needs a regular supply of protein to generate energy and replace tissue. For vegetarians, who cannot eat meat and fish, protein-rich foods include soybeans, 40% protein, nuts, seeds and beans, 30% protein. Meat, on the other hand, contains only 20% usable protein.

### 2. Carbohydrates

Although blamed as the most fattening of foods, carbohydrates, mostly burnt as the body's fuel, provide heat and energy, and are a very useful source of other nutrients, such as vitamins and minerals. For vegetarians, some of the main sources of carbohydrates are grains, herbs, sugars, corn, fruits, and potatoes.

## 3. Fat

Fats produce about twice as much energy as carbohydrates. During digestion, they are broken down into glycerol and fatty acids, which are required for growth and healthy cell development. They can be found in vegetable oils, milk, butter, peanuts, etc. Natural vegetable oils contain certain essential fats that cannot be obtained by eating meat, and they do not contain any harmful cholesterol.

## 4. Vitamins

Even though they are present in most food in small quantities, serious health problems can arise from deficiency. Many vegetables have high vitamin contents. The sources and functions of important vitamins are listed in the table below.

| Vitamin | Source | Benefit |
|---------|--------|---------|
| Vitamin A | Butter, margarine, carrots, spinach, watercress and apricots | Aids growth and protects moist tissue in the eyes, throat and lungs. |
| Vitamin B Complex | Bread, milk and dairy products, yeast and green leafy vegetables | Assists in converting food into usable materials for body building or energy. |
| Vitamin C | Oranges, lemons, chillies, black currants, peppers, cauliflower, potatoes, peas, cabbage, spinach, and watercress | Aids healing and resistance to infection and keeps connective tissues in good repair. Aids in the assimilation of iron. |
| Vitamin D | Margarine, eggs, butter | Aids healthy bone development. |

**Source:** The Vegetarian Gourmet, Judy Ridgeway. Englewood Cliff, NJ, Prentice-Hall (1981), p.6

## 5. Minerals

Minerals perform various important functions in the body, acting as the essential elements for almost all of its chemical reactions, allowing the transmission of nervous impulses and aiding digestion. About one fourth of the body's magnesium and one fifth of its iron are provided by fruits, vegetables and dairy products.

## 6. Water

Water is essential for a variety of body processes.

After looking at these six types of nutrients, you will no longer need to ask the question, "**Will I get enough nutrition without eating meat?**"

## Delicious & Nutritious

"Your food shall be your remedies,
and your remedies shall be your foods."

- Hippocrates, the Father of Medicine

A vegetarian diet is more natural for the human body and easier to digest. Vegetarian nutrition and good eating habits also enhance physical fitness and lead to a longer life.

Please understand that eating less does not mean starving yourself, it simply means taking in fewer calories. The first step for vegetarians is to reduce your meat intake by eating more fruits, vegetables and dairy products.

Begin your new eating habits with attention, care and love. It is not beyond your ability. Selecting your food means selecting the kind of life you want to live. Cooking for yourself may be another solution. You'll be surprised to find that learning to cook vegetarian food is easy; easier than you might think.

Then you will find that eating a vegetarian diet, the natural diet for human beings, does the least harm to the earth's living creatures, and also helps increase our awareness of the unity and harmony of life.

References:
1. The Vegetarian Gourmet, Judy Ridge. Englewood Cliff, NJ, Prentice-Hall (1981)
2. Nutrition Qualities of Fresh Fruits and Vegetables, Phillip White, Mount Kisco, NY, Futura Pub. (1974)
3. The Vegetable Passion, Janet Barkas, NY, Scribner (1975)
4. The Encyclopedia Americana, International Edition, Connecticut, Grolier Incorporated (1991)

# YAM SHANGHIA
## MUNG BEAN SHEET SALAD

### INGREDIENTS:
1 cup mung bean sheet pieces, soaked
1/4 cup soaked ear mushrooms, shredded
1/4 cup carrot strips of 1" length
1/4 cup firm white bean curd, cut lengthwise into
strips to be deep fried.
1/4 cup chinese lily buds, soaked and knotted
1/4 cup bell pepper strips of 1" length
1/4 cup baby corn (sliced diagonally)

### PREPARATION:

Bring a pot of water to boil. Immerse baby corn,
mung bean sheets, ear mushrooms, lily buds
and carrot strips. Cook for 1 minute.
Remove with a perforated spoon
and place contents into a mixing bowl.
Deep fry bean curd strips until golden.
Drain fried bean curd strips and add to above
ingredients along with bell pepper strips.

### SAUCE
### INGREDIENTS:

3 tbsp lime juice
2 hot chillies (smashed)
2 tbsp soy sauce
2 tbsp vegetable oil
1/4 tsp salt
2 tbsp sugar
lettuce, cilantro sprigs, and chilli strips for garnish.

### PREPARATION:

In a small bowl, mix lime juice, hot chillies,
soy sauce, vegetable oil, salt and sugar together.
Stir until sugar dissolves.
Pour sauce over vegetables in mixing bowl
and toss well.

Arrange lettuce on a plate and top with salad.
Garnish with cilantro sprigs and chilli strips
before serving.
**SERVES 4.**

# HED SOD SAI
## STUFFED MUSHROOMS

### INGREDIENTS:
20 fresh mushrooms, clean, remove stalks and gills
1 cup soft white bean curd, mashed
2 tbsp finely diced onions
4 tbsp finely diced bell pepper
4 tbsp finely diced carrots
4 tbsp green peas
3 tbsp chopped whole kernel corn
3 tbsp finely diced water chestnuts
1 egg
1/2 tsp salt
2 tsp Maggi sauce
2 tsp sesame oil
3 tbsp corn flour
2 tsp sugar

### PREPARATION:
In a bowl, mix bean curd, onions, bell peppers, carrots,
green peas, chopped corn and diced water chestnuts.
Season with salt, Maggi sauce,
sesame oil, sugar, egg and corn flour.
Mix well and spoon mixture into cleaned mushrooms.

### FLOUR BATTER
### INGREDIENTS:
1/4 cup corn flour
1/4 cup wheat flour
2 tsp baking powder
1/2 tsp salt
1/4 cup cold water
1/4 cup evaporated milk

### PREPARATION:
Sift together corn flour, wheat flour, baking powder
and salt. Slowly add cold water and evaporated milk
stirring into a smooth paste. Strain mixture before use.
Prepare a wok half full of oil.
Dip stuffed mushrooms into flour batter
and deep fry until golden and crisp.
Drain and place on a serving plate.

### SAUCE
### INGREDIENTS:
1 tbsp chopped garlic
1 tbsp chopped shallots
1/4 cup vegetable oil
2 tbsp sugar
1 tbsp chilli sauce
2 tbsp tomato sauce
1 tbsp rice vinegar
1/4 tsp salt
1 tbsp white wine

### PREPARATION:
Fry onions and garlic in vegetable oil
until golden and fragrant.
Mix in tomato sauce, sugar, chilli sauce, vinegar,
salt and lastly white wine.
Let mixture boil and remove from stove.
Serve with fried mushrooms
**SERVES 8.**

# TAU HOO NENG
## STEAMED BEAN CURD

### INGREDIENTS:
2 cups soft white bean curd (minced)
1/4 cup egg whites
1/4 tsp salt
4 tbsp wheat flour
1/4 tsp ground pepper
4 ear mushrooms (soak and shred)
2 red chillies (de-seed and shred)
1/2 cup bell pepper (cut to strips of 1" length)

### PREPARATION:
In a bowl, mix bean curd, egg whites, salt,
wheat flour and ground pepper together.

Arrange small amounts of chilli strips,
bell pepper and ear mushroom shreds
in a small individual ramekin and
press minced bean curd mixture over it.
Do the same for the rest of the mixture.

Steam over high heat for 10 mins.
Cool for 5 mins before removing from ramekin.
Arrange bean curd on a serving dish.

### SAUCE
### INGREDIENTS:
1 tbsp chopped garlic
1 cup vegetable stock
2 tbsp finely diced carrots
2 tsp soy sauce
2 tsp Maggi Sauce
2 tsp sugar
1 tbsp corn flour
1 tbsp vegetable oil
1 tbsp water
cilantro sprigs and roughly ground
pepper for garnish

### PREPARATION:
Dilute corn flour with water and set aside.
In a small frying pan, fry chopped garlic with 1 tbsp
vegetable oil until golden. Mix in green peas, carrots
and vegetable stock. Bring to boil and add corn flour
and water mixture.

Season with soy sauce, sugar and Maggi sauce.
Boil until sauce thickens.

Pour thickened hot sauce over bean curd.
Garnish with cilantro sprigs
and ground pepper.

### SERVES 4.

# POH PIAH THOD
## DEEP FRIED SPRING ROLLS

### INGREDIENTS:
30 spring roll sheets of 7" diameter
1/4 cup diced fresh mushrooms
1/4 cup ear mushrooms (soak and shred)
1 cup taro root shreds of 1" length
1/2 cup mung bean noodles
(soaked and cut to 1" length)
3 tbsp green peas
1/2 cup firm white bean curd (cut to 1" strips)
1/4 cup carrot strips of 1" length
1 tbsp chopped garlic
1 tbsp Maggi sauce
2 tsp soy sauce
1/2 tsp salt
1 tsp ground pepper
1 tbsp sugar
egg whites for sealing rolls
vegetable oil for deep frying

### PREPARATION:
Prepare a wok with 3 tbsp vegetable oil and fry
chopped garlic till golden. Add in diced fresh
mushrooms, taro root, mung bean noodles, green peas,
ear mushrooms, bean curd and carrot strips.
Stir fry vegetables over high heat for 1 min.

Season with Maggi sauce,
soy sauce, salt, pepper and sugar.
Remove filling and cool before wrapping
with spring roll sheets.

Place 2 tbsp filling onto a spring roll sheet and brush
the edges with egg white. Fold both ends towards the
filling and roll up tight into a cylinder.
Seal with egg whites again.

Half fill a wok with vegetable oil and
deep-fry spring rolls in medium hot oil until golden.
Drain and arrange on a serving plate.

### SAUCE
### INGREDIENTS:
1/2 cup rice vinegar
1/2 cup sugar
1/2 tsp salt
2 red chillies (de-seed and slice)
1 tbsp sliced garlic
2 tbsp roasted ground peanuts
cilantro sprigs for garnish

### PREPARATION:
In a mortar, pound garlic and chillies to a fine paste.

In a small pot, mix sugar, salt, vinegar. Bring to a boil.
Add in ground chilli paste and bring to boil again.
Remove from stove and garnish with ground peanuts
and cilantro sprigs. Serve with spring rolls.

### SERVES 10.

# KAPAO KROP KHAI HOR
## OMELETTE WITH CRISP BASIL LEAVES

### INGREDIENTS:
2 eggs
2 tsp lime juice
2 tbsp corn flour + 1 tbsp water
1 tbsp chopped garlic
3 tbsp diced ginko nuts
2 tbsp cleaned lotus seeds
1/4 cup abalone mushrooms (cut into strips)
2 tbsp diced gluten (see page 214)
1/4 cup diced firm white bean curd
2 tbsp chopped water chestnuts
2 tbsp green peas
2 tbsp diced carrots
5 diced champignon mushrooms
2 hot chillies (smashed)
2 tbsp vegetable oil
1 tbsp Maggi sauce
2 tsp soy sauce
2 tsp sugar
1/2 cup deep fried basil leaves (kapao)

### PREPARATION:
In a wok, fry chopped garlic with
vegetable oil till golden.

Add in ginko nuts, lotus seeds, abalone
mushrooms, gluten, bean curd, water chestnuts
green peas, carrots, diced champignons and hot
chillies. Stir fry over high heat till cooked,
about 2 mins.
Season with Maggi sauce, soy sauce and sugar.
Remove mixture and cool before use.

In a small bowl, break eggs and mix with lime
juice. Add corn flour mixture and mix well.

With 3 tbsp vegetable oil in wok, fry omelette
swirling pan to get an evenly thin omelette.
Cook over low heat till evenly golden.

Place omelette on a serving plate. Fill omelette
with vegetable mixture and fold in half.
Garnish with fried basil leaves and serve.

### SERVES 4.

# TAKAR BENJALONG
## RAINBOW BASKET

### INGREDIENTS:
2 cups cooked Chinese noodles
1/2 cup diced celery
1/4 cup diced tomatoes
1/4 cup diced onions
1/4 cup diced bell peppers
1/4 cup diced champignon mushrooms
1/4 cup diced pineapple
1/2 cup roasted cashew nuts for garnish
vegetable oil for deep frying

### PREPARATION:
Half fill a wok with vegetable oil.

Arrange cooked Chinese
noodles in a 3" strainer.
Place a smaller perforated spoon on top of
noodles to prevent them from floating around.
Deep fry noodle basket till basket turns golden.
Remove and place basket on a serving plate.

Drain oil from wok. Replace with 2 tbsp oil in
wok and fry onions till soft. Add celery,
tomatoes, bell peppers, champignons and
pineapple. Fry over high heat for 1 min.
Remove vegetables from wok and spoon into a
small mixing bowl.

### SAUCE
### INGREDIENTS:
1/2 cup rice vinegar
1/2 cup sugar
1/2 tsp salt
2 red chillies (de-seed and slice)
1 tbsp sliced garlic
1/4 cup tomato puree

### PREPARATION:
In a mortar pound chillies and garlic
to a fine paste.

In a small pot, mix sugar, vinegar and salt
together. Bring to boil and add in ground chilli
paste and tomato puree. Bring to boil again.
Toss vegetables and sauce together and
spoon into crisp baskets.
Garnish with cashew nuts and cilantro sprigs.

### SERVES 4.

# NAM YA HED FANG
## MUSHROOM SAUCE

**INGREDIENTS FOR SPICE MIXTURE:**

1/4 cup soaked dried chillies
1 tsp salt
2 tsp galangal
2 tbsp sliced lemon grass
1/4 cup sliced shallots
1/4 cup sliced garlic
1/4 cup krachai (remove brown skin and cut
into pieces)
1/4 cup water

**PREPARATION:**

In a food processor, mix the above spices
together and blend till smooth.
Set aside for later use.

**OTHER INGREDIENTS:**

2 tbsp vegetable oil
1 cup thick coconut milk
3 cups light coconut milk
2 cups sliced straw mushrooms
2 tsp salt
1 tbsp soy sauce
1 tbsp palm sugar

**PREPARATION:**

In a food processor, mix straw mushrooms and
light coconut milk together. Blend till smooth.
In a pot, fry spice mixture with vegetable oil over
low heat till fragrant.

Add mushroom mixture to spice mixture
and bring to boil. Add soy sauce, salt and
palm sugar. Bring to boil. Add thick coconut
milk. Bring to boil and remove from stove.

To be served with vegetables and pasta.
Arrange cooked pasta on a serving plate with
cooked yard long beans, bean sprouts, olives,
deep-fried hot chillies and serve with
hot mushroom sauce.

**SERVES 4.**

# KHAO TAU HOO YEE
# KAP MU WAN TIAM
## VEGETARIAN RICE WITH GLUTEN SWEET PORK

**INGREDIENTS:**

2 cups cooked rice
2 tbsp vegetable oil
1 tbsp fermented red bean curd
2 tsp hot chillies
2 tsp garlic
1 tbsp fermented soy beans
1 tbsp sugar

**PREPARATION:**

In a mortar, pound hot chillies, garlic and
fermented soy beans to a paste.
Add fermented red bean curd and mix well.

In a frying pan, fry ground paste with
vegetable oil till fragrant.
Mix in rice and sugar.
Toss rice till well mixed and remove from stove.

Place rice on a plate to be served with sweet
gluten pork and vegetables.

**GLUTEN SWEET PORK**
**INGREDIENTS:**

2 cups gluten (cut into pieces), see page 214
1/2 cup palm sugar
2 tbsp vegetable oil
2 sliced shallots
1 tbsp Maggi sauce
1/2 tsp salt
vegetable oil for deep-frying
green mango shreds, carrot shreds, finely sliced
yard long beans, lime slices and shredded
omelette for garnish.

**PREPARATION:**

Half fill a wok with vegetable oil. Deep fry
gluten pieces til crisp, remove for later use.
Drain wok and replace with 2 tbsp oil and fry
shallots till slightly brown and fragrant.

Mix in fried gluten and season with salt
and Maggi sauce.

Remove from stove and serve with rice
and fresh vegetables.
**SERVES 2.**

## TAO HOO NAM DAENG
### BEAN CURD STEW

**INGREDIENTS:**
1/4  cup white fungus
(soaked and cut to florets)
1/4  cup diced carrots
1/4  cup diced bell peppers
1/4  cup sliced baby corn
2  cakes firm white bean curd
(cut to 2" x 2" pieces)
2  tsp chopped onions
2  tbsp vegetable oil
1  cup vegetable stock
1/2  tsp salt
2  tbsp chilli sauce
2  tbsp tomato sauce
2  tsp sugar
2  tsp soy sauce
1  tbsp corn flour
1  tbsp water

**PREPARATION:**
Dilute corn flour with water
and keep for later use.

Microwave bean curd at full power for 1 min and
arrange on a serving plate.

In a frying pan, fry onions with vegetable oil till
soft and fragrant. Add vegetable stock. Bring to
boil and season with salt, chilli sauce,
tomato sauce, sugar and soy sauce.

Stir in corn flour mixture.
Mix in white fungus, diced carrots, bell peppers
and sliced baby corn. Boil until sauce thickens
Remove from stove.
Pour hot gravy over beancurd and serve.

**SERVES 2.**

## BARBECUE MONGSAWIRAT
### VEGETARIAN KEBABS

**INGREDIENTS:**
20  whole champignon mushrooms
20  pieces 1" x 1" bell peppers
20  1" x 1" firm white bean curd squares
20  1" x 1" gluten pieces (see page 214)
20  1" x 1" diced carrots
20  1" x 1" diced pineapple
20  cherry tomatoes
20  sweet basil leaves (horapha)
10  wooden skewers

**PREPARATION:**
With wooden skewers, string the above
ingredients together and brush with
soft margarine.

Grill kebabs till cooked and serve with
barbecue sauce.

**BARBECUE SAUCE
INGREDIENTS:**
1/4  cup red curry paste
1/2  cup creamy peanut butter
2  tbsp margarine
1  cup evaporated milk
1  cup coconut milk
1/2  tsp salt
4  tbsp sugar
4  tbsp roasted ground white sesame seeds

**PREPARATION:**
In a frying pan, fry margarine with curry paste
and peanut butter over low fire till fragrant.

Mix in coconut milk and evaporated milk.
Boil till thickened.

Season with salt, sugar and
ground sesame seeds.
Remove from stove and brush sauce on kebabs.

**SERVES 10.**

# YAM SAM SAR
## RICE VERMICELLI SALAD

### INGREDIENTS:
1 cup soaked rice vermicelli
2 tbsp roasted cashew nuts
1 tbsp young ginger strips
1 cake diced firm white bean curd
1/4 cup champignon mushrooms (cut in half)
1 tbsp soaked ear mushrooms (shred)
1 tbsp carrot strips
1/4 cup cooked broccoli (cut to florets)

### PREPARATION:
Prepare a pot of water and bring to boil.
Cook rice vermicelli till soft.
Drain with a perforated spoon.

Arrange rice vermicelli on a serving plate
with ginger strips, bean curd, mushrooms,
carrots and broccoli.

Serve with hot sauce.

### SAUCE
### INGREDIENTS:
1 tbsp vegetable oil
1 tbsp pounded red chilli
2 tbsp lime juice
2 tbsp sugar
2 tbsp soy sauce

### PREPARATION:
Mix the sauce ingredients together in
a small mixing bowl.
Stir till sugar dissolves and serve
with rice vermicelli.

### SERVES 4.

# PHAT PHAK SEE YU HOM
## STIR-FRIED VEGETABLES
## IN SOY SAUCE

### INGREDIENTS:
1/4 cup sliced baby corn
1/4 cup sliced fresh mushrooms
1/4 cup broccoli (cut to florets)
1/4 cup sliced carrots
1 tbsp chopped garlic
3 tbsp vegetable oil
2 tsp Maggi sauce
2 tsp soy sauce
1/4 tsp salt
2 tsp sugar
2 tbsp vegetable stock

### PREPARATION:
In a frying pan, fry chopped garlic with
vegetable oil till fragrant.

Mix in baby corn, fresh mushrooms,
broccoli and sliced carrots. Fry over high
heat for another 1 min.

Add in vegetable stock and season with soy
sauce, Maggi sauce, salt and sugar.
Remove from stove.

Arrange on a serving plate and
garnish with cilantro sprigs.

### SERVES 4.

# SOUP CANTALOPE
## CANTALOUPE SOUP

### INGREDIENTS:
1/4  cup diced champignon mushrooms
1 cantaloupe (cleaned)
1/4  cup diced gluten (see page 214)
1 tbsp young ginger strips
1 1/2 cups soft white bean curd,
cut into 1" cubes
5  soaked dried shiitake mushrooms (sliced)
1/4  cup cooked peanuts
1 tsp sesame oil
1 tbsp vegetable oil
3 cups vegetable stock
1 tbsp soy sauce
1/4 tsp salt
chopped spring onion for garnish

### PREPARATION:
Cut cantaloupe 2" from top and hollow out .
Carve cantaloupe and lid.

In a frying pan, heat sesame oil and vegetable
oil together. Fry ginger till fragrant.
Add in gluten, sliced shiitake mushrooms,
and diced champignons.
Add vegetable stock and
bring to boil.

Add peanuts and bean curd.
Season with soy sauce and salt.
Bring to boil.
Remove from stove.
Ladle soup into hollowed out
cantaloupe and cover with lid.
Steam cantaloupe over high heat  for 10 mins.
Remove from stove and serve hot.

### SERVES 4.

# KHAO OP SAPPAROD
## PINEAPPLE RICE

### INGREDIENTS:
1  cup cooked rice
1 pineapple (2 lb size)
2 tbsp green peas
2 tbsp diced carrots
3  soaked dried shiitake mushrooms (sliced)
1/4  cup diced pineapple (scooped from
pineapple)
1/4  cup sliced gluten
1/4  cup diced onion
1 tbsp raisins
1 tbsp sultanas
1/4  cup diced tomatoes
1/4  cup roasted cashew nuts
5  pitted olives
1 tbsp Maggi sauce
1 tbsp sugar
1/4  tsp salt
1 tbsp soy sauce
1/2 tsp ground pepper
3 tbsp vegetable oil
fresh chilli strips and cilantro
sprigs for garnish

### PREPARATION:
Clean and cut pineapple lengthwise into halves.
Hollow pineapple to about 1/2" from skin.
Dice removed pineapple
meat into cubes for later use.

In a frying pan, with 3 tbsp vegetable oil, fry
onions till soft and fragrant. Add sliced
mushrooms, green peas, carrots, gluten and rice.
Stir-fry for 2 mins over high heat.
Stir in raisins, sultanas,
diced tomatoes and pineapple.

Season with Maggi sauce, sugar, salt, soy suace
and pepper. Remove from stove and ladle rice
into hollowed pineapple halves.
Toss in olives and cashew nuts.

Cover filled pineapples with aluminium foil
and bake in hot oven for 15 mins.
Remove from oven and garnish with
chilli shreds and cilantro sprigs.

### SERVES 4.

# TAO HOO OP MOR DIN
## CLAY POT BEAN CURD

### INGREDIENTS:

1/4 cup sliced gluten (see page 214)
1 cup fried firm white bean curd of 1" length
1/4 cup diced champignon mushrooms
1/4 cup cooked red kidney beans
2 tbsp green peas
3 tbsp sliced young ginger
2 tsp chopped garlic
2 tbsp vegetable oil
2 tbsp Maggi sauce
1 tbsp sugar
2 tsp soy sauce
1 cup vegetable stock
2 fresh chillies (de-seed and cut into strips)
sweet basil leaves (horapha) for garnish

### PREPARATION:

In a wok, fry garlic in vegetable oil till golden.
Mix in sliced gluten, fried bean curd,
diced mushrooms, red kidney beans,
green peas and ginger. Stir-fry for 1 min.

Add vegetable stock and season with
Maggi sauce, sugar and soy sauce.
Remove from stove.

Pour mixture into claypot and cover.
Simmer over low heat for 20 mins.
Remove from stove and garnish with chillies
and sweet basil leaves.

### SERVES 4.

# MEE KROP MANGSAWIRAT
## VEGETARIAN MEE KROP

### INGREDIENTS:

4 cups soaked rice vermicelli
1/4 cup deep fried firm white
bean curd of 1" length
2 tsp chopped garlic
2 tsp sliced shallots
2 tbsp rice vinegar
1/2 tsp salt
1/4 cup tomato sauce
2 tbsp chilli sauce
vegetable oil for deep-frying
cilantro sprigs, chilli strips, bean sprouts,
carrot strips, fried shallots and
pickled garlic for garnish.

### PREPARATION:

Half fill a wok with vegetable oil. Deep-fry
small amounts of the rice vermicelli in
moderately hot oil till crisp.
Drain with a perforated spoon and set aside.

Drain oil from wok and refill with 2 tbsp oil.
Fry garlic and shallots till golden. Add palm
sugar and cook till sugar dissolves and thickens.
Add tomato sauce, vinegar, salt and chilli sauce.
Toss in fried beancurd strips.
Remove from stove.
Pour gravy over crisp vermicelli and toss well.
Garnish with fresh vegetables and serve.

### SERVES 2.

# TOM YAM ROD SAP
## HOT & SOUR VEGETARIAN SOUP

### INGREDIENTS:
1/4  cup champignon mushrooms
(cut into halves)
1/4  cup japanese golden mushrooms (enoki)
1/4  cup sliced fresh wild mushrooms
4  kaffir lime leaves (torn)
2  slices galangal
2  3" pieces lemon grass (smashed)
2  3" lengths coriander root
2  shallots (smashed)
3  cups vegetable stock
1/4  cup evaporated milk
1  tsp salt
2  tbsp soy sauce
4  tbsp roasted chilli paste (nam phrik phao)
1  tbsp sugar
4  tbsp lime juice
1  tbsp hot chillies (smashed)
cilantro sprigs and
deep-fried hot chillies for garnish

### PREPARATION:
In a medium pot, add kaffir lime leaves,
galangal, coriander roots, shallots,
lemon grass and vegetable stock.
Bring to boil for 10 mins.

Add all mushrooms and bring to boil again.
Season with salt, soy sauce, roasted chilli paste
and sugar.

Add evaporated milk, lime juice and hot chillies.
Bring to full boil and remove from stove.
Spoon into a serving bowl.
Garnish with cilantro sprigs and fried chillies.

### SERVES 4.

# THOD MAN VITAMIN
## SAVORY VEGETARIAN FRITTERS

### INGREDIENTS:
1 tbsp rice flour
2 cups wheat flour
1 cup water
1/2 tsp baking powder
1 tbsp sugar
1 tsp ground pepper
2 tsp salt
1 tsp sesame oil
1 tbsp vegetable oil
1/2 cup green peas
1/4  cup soaked dried shiitake mushrooms (diced)
1/2  cup diced carrots
1/4  cup roasted cashew nuts (chopped)
1/4  cup diced celery
1/2  cup diced baby corn
1/2  cup diced gluten (deep-fried till crisp)

### PREPARATION:
Mix rice flour, wheat flour, baking powder, sugar,
ground pepper and salt together.

Slowly, add water and mix into a smooth paste. Add in
sesame oil and vegetable oil.

Mix in green peas, diced mushrooms, carrots,
cashew nuts, celery, baby corn and fried gluten.

In a wok, fill oil till half full and deep fry batter 1 tbsp
at a time over moderately hot oil till golden.

Drain and arrange thod man on a serving plate to be
served with sauce and vegetable relish.

### SAUCE
### INGREDIENTS:
1/4  cup red chillies (cut to pieces)
3 tbsp garlic
1 tsp salt
1/2  cup rice vinegar
1/2  cup sugar

### PREPARATION:
Pound red chillies, garlic and salt in a mortar till fine.

Mix the ground chilli paste in a small pot and bring to
boil  with vinegar and sugar. When mixture thickens,
remove from stove.

### VEGETABLE RELISH
### INGREDIENTS:
1 cup cucumber (remove core and slice)
1 cup sliced carrots
1 cup cauliflower (cut to florets)
1 cup rice vinegar
1 cup sugar
2 cups water
2 tsp salt

### PREPARATION:
In a pyrex dish add 1 tbsp salt to sliced cucumber and
carrots and mix well. Place salted vegetables in a piece
of muslin cloth to remove excess water. Return to
pyrex dish and add cauliflower.

Bring vinegar, sugar, salt and water to a boil in a small
pot. Cool and pour over vegetables. Cover pyrex dish
and refrigerate. Serve with thod man.
### SERVES 6.

# THE VEGETARIAN FESTIVAL

Most old Chinese temples in Thailand, normally calm and peaceful, are crowded with people today. Scores of joss sticks burn slowly on the altar, the light from hundreds of white candles dances in the dimness. The main hall is heavy with the fragrance of incense, and the smoke is so thick that your eyes are easily irritated. An old Thai-Chinese woman dressed in white beside you murmurs softly; she is probably praying to the gods for happiness and prosperity for her family and children.

**The Vegetarian Festival** has arrived once again, and thousands of Thais have flocked to Phuket to witness its ancient rituals and experience mystical ceremonies that cannot be explained by scientists.

Every year, more and more Thais attend the annual vegetarian festival, held from the first to the ninth day of the ninth lunar month. The festival in Phuket is especially popular, bringing together almost all of the local people hand-in-hand to participate in the religious rites.

People flow into the city from nearby areas and from remote provinces. Every kind of accommodation is booked solid for the entire nine days. Most restaurants raise yellow flags to indicate that only vegetarian food will be served. Phuket turns into a virgin land.

**Legend**

**The Vegetarian Festival** symbolizes the journey of nine respected gods, Kao Ong Ear or Kao Ong Tai Te, on their visit from heaven to earth. No one knows when the

39

festival was first held, but it is known to have occurred in China as early as the reign of Emperor Houng Te, about 1500 B.C. Its primary objective is to encourage purification of both body and mind.

In Thailand the festival was first practiced in Phuket Island more than 100 years ago. Most of the island's inhabitants at the time were Chinese laborers who had immigrated to Siam to work in tin mines. During the reign of **King Rama V,** there were more than 30,000 such laborers working on Phuket and in neighboring provinces.

The mining business was very successful, and the Chinese community expanded rapidly. To make money, a Chinese opera troupe was brought in from China to entertain them. In addition to their cultural and artistic performances, they introduced **The Vegetarian Festival** to Siam for the first time. Local Phuket people followed their teachings and devotion to the festival.

But the opera troupe did not know every detail of how to conduct the ritual, so a group of Thais donated and collected money to send some of the players back to China to record and study the correct method. One year passed and then two years, but the opera players did not return. The Thais began to believe thay had been cheated.

Finally, in the third year, they sailed into Phuket port with the complete record and a holy incense pot with three joss sticks that had been burning all the way

from China. Thus **the vegetarian festival** began in Phuket, and it has continued ever since, expanding to neighboring provinces and countries.

### Reckoning The Rites

The ceremony traditionally takes nine days, but it is flexible, so that people can choose to participate for a shorter period of time: one, three or five days. During the holy ceremony, faithful followers dress in white and let their hair down. The participants will observe eight of the ten Buddhist precepts, such as no sexual intercourse, cosmetics or perfume.

The food must be meatless and cooked in vegetable oil. The cooking equipment must be clean or new, specially separated from normal use. Most people will eat in the temples or take food home by paying money to the temples for three meals a day- a total of about $20 per person for the entire nine days.

The food is extremely tasty, reflecting the creativity of the local people. Beginning with breakfast: boiled rice with salty fried peanuts, pickles, sweet bean cakes, etc. Following that with lunch, composed of rice or noodles and four or five kinds of dishes, such as curry, sour salad, fried vegetables or vegetable soup. Finish the day with a dinner of rice and three other dishes.

Visit Phuket for the festival and try the food; you'll discover a new definition of delicious.

The festival usually falls in early **October.** The day before it begins, the temples are cleaned up and smoked with incense. At night, a big bamboo pole with nine oil lamps(Ko Teng) is raised to welcome the arrival of the deities and to pronounce the beginning of the festival.

On the First day, people bring fruit to the temples to pay homage to the gods. The vegetarians will be called Cheng on the third day-meaning cleanliness and purity. On the sixth day, the protection rite, Bang koon, is prepared to prevent the devil from breaking the ceremony and harming its participants. On the seventh day, the stars are worshipped and asked for glory and happiness; on the eighth day, a procession travels around the city to commemorate the incense pot's arrival from mainland China.Around midnight of the last day, the procession makes its way to the port to bid farewell to the gods and send them back to heaven.

Chinese firecrackers explode to signify the end of the vegetarian festival.

And life returns to normal.

### Faith & Enigma

If people have faith in something, they will devote all their energy and soul to achieve it. During **the vegetarian festival,** participants in the rites strongly believe that the gods will protect them. Gods and spirits are invited to possess the mediums, who are believed to be fated to die soon. They are selected to sacrifice their lives by means of self-torture, walking on blazing coals and climbing on the blades of sharp knives.

On the last day of the ritual, the mediums show the power of deities by performing certain acts of self-torture. They pierce their cheeks with sharp steel rods and suspend objects such as apples and oranges on either side of the rod. To the astonishment of all present, after removing the rod, there is no blood or scar. Even when stuck with nails, knives, axes or a pin pendulum, their skin shows only minor scratches.

Imagine a large pile of burning charcoal so hot that people have to step back from its heat and fumes. The mediums simply walk on the fire as if they were walking on the beach. Who are they? Some participants who believe that they are clean-children, woman and the elderly excepted-are permitted to follow the mediums. Nothing happens to them.

The mediums perform another challenging feat. Thirty-six sharp knife blades are arranged like stairs; merely the reflection of the sharpened blades screams, "Do not even think of touching me." But the mediums cry out and climb to the top without hesitation. Then they climb back down to the ground; a total of 72 steps. As you might expect by now, they arrive unhurt and unscathed.

These rituals may seem incredible. You may ask yourself whether these men are actually spirit mediums or just magicians playing tricks. There are some things that are beyond scientific explanation. As time passes, the vegetarian festival, with all its mystery, continues to receive more and more attention from all walks of life.

**Come to Phuket and experience it with your own eyes**.

**THE RITE IS STILL ALIVE.
THE MYSTERY IS STILL MYSTIC.**

# PHAT PHAK PASOM
## STIR FRIED RAINBOW VEGETABLES

### INGREDIENTS:
1/4 cup diced bell peppers
1/4 cup tomatoes, cut into wedges
1/4 cup diced cooked potatoes
1/4 cup boiled cauliflower cut into florets
1/4 cup diced cooked carrots
1/4 cup straw mushrooms (cut to halves)
1/4 cup diced firm white bean curd
1/4 cup cooked shell macaroni
1/4 cup watercress
2 tbsp green peas
2 tbsp sliced shallots
4 tbsp vegetable stock
1 tsp salt
2 tsp sugar
1 tsp ground pepper
1 tbsp Maggi sauce
2 tsp soy sauce
2 tbsp vegetable oil

### PREPARATION:
In a frying pan, fry shallots in vegetable oil till
slightly brown and fragrant.

Add in potatoes, cauliflower, tomatoes,
bell peppers, diced carrots, straw mushrooms,
bean curd and watercress.
Stir-fry over high heat
for 1 min.

Season with salt, sugar, ground pepper,
Maggi sauce, soy sauce and vegetable stock.
Stir-fry for 30 secs over high heat and arrange on
a serving plate.

### SERVES 4.

# HOI JOR NAM JIM BUOI
## "SEAFOOD" ROLLS WITH PLUM SAUCE

### INGREDIENTS:
3 bean curd sheets (8" square)
1/2 cup carrot strips of 1 1/2" length
1/4 cup soaked dried shiitake mushrooms
(chopped)
1/2 cup cooked peanuts
1/4 cup chopped gluten (see page 214)
1/4 cup egg whites
2 tbsp corn flour
2 tbsp wheat flour
3 cups taro root strips of 1 1/2" lengths
1 tbsp soy sauce
1 tbsp Maggi sauce
1 tbsp sugar
1 tsp ground pepper
1 tbsp chopped garlic
vegetable oil for deep-frying

### PREPARATION:
In a frying pan, fry chopped garlic
with oil till golden.
Add chopped mushrooms and gluten.
Fry over high heat for 30 secs.
Remove from stove.

In a small bowl, mix mushroom mixture with
carrots, peanuts and taro root strips.
Mix in egg whites, corn flour, and wheat flour.
Season with soy sauce, Maggi sauce, sugar,
salt and ground pepper. Mix well.

Divide mixture into 3 portions and place 1
portion on each of the bean curd sheets
and roll up into a cylinder.
Knot the cylinder roll into 8 portions.

Prick all over with a needle and steam over high
heat till cooked, about 10 mins.
Cool rolls and cut into pieces through knots.

In a wok, fill oil till half full and fry hoi jor
(seafood rolls) in moderately
hot oil till golden and crisp.

Remove from oil and drain. Arrange on a serving
plate with fresh vegetables.
Serve with chinese plum sauce.
### SERVES 4.

# TOM KHA JEA
## OMELETTE IN SPICY COCONUT SOUP

### INGREDIENTS:
2 eggs (beaten)
2 tbsp vegetable oil
1 cup abalone mushrooms (cut into halves)
1/4 cup evaporated milk
1 cup coconut milk
1 cup vegetable stock
1 tbsp hot chillies (smashed)
2 shallots (smashed)
3 kaffir lime leaves (torn)
10 slices galangal
1/2 tsp salt
2 tbsp soy sauce
1 tbsp sugar
1 tbsp roasted chilli paste (nam phrik phao)
3 tbsp lime juice
cilantro sprigs and
deep-fried chillies for garnish

### PREPARATION:
In a frying pan, fry beaten eggs with vegetable oil till cooked and cut into pieces.

In a pot, mix coconut milk, evaporated milk, vegetable stock, smashed hot chillies, kaffir lime leaves, shallots and galangal.

Bring mixture to boil for 5 mins.
Season with salt, soy sauce and sugar.

Add in cut omelette pieces, abalone mushrooms, roasted chilli paste and lime juice. Let mixture boil again and remove from stove.

Garnish with cilantro sprigs and fried chillies before serving.

### SERVES 4.

# SAM RIAM
# SAMOSA

### INGREDIENTS:
20 spring roll sheets of 2" x 6" strips
1 cup diced cooked potatoes
1/4 cup diced cooked carrots
2 hard boiled eggs (cut into chunks)
1/4 cup chopped onions
1/4 cup green peas
1/2 cup coconut milk
1 tsp salt
2 tbsp sugar
1 tbsp curry powder
2 tsp ground pepper
1/4 cup diced gluten (see page 214)
4 tbsp wheat flour
2 tbsp vegetable oil
egg whites for sealing
vegetable oil for deep-frying

### PREPARATION:
In a frying pan, with 2 tbsp vegetable oil, fry onions till fragrant. Add in gluten, potatoes, carrots and green peas.

Stir-fry for 1 min, add coconut milk and boil.
Season with salt, sugar, and ground pepper
Add curry powder and wheat flour.
Cook till mixture thickens.
Remove from stove and cool before using.

Place 1 tbsp of filling onto one end of spring roll skin.
Top with a chuck of hard boil egg and fold into a triangular shape, sealing with egg whites.

In a wok, fill vegetable oil till 1/2 full and deep-fry samosas in moderately hot oil till golden and crisp.
Drain and serve with sauce.

### SERVES 10.

# KAENG JUED JEA
## VEGETARIAN SOUP

### INGREDIENTS:
1 tsp salted radish (tang chye)
1/4 cup mung bean noodles (soaked
and cut to 2" lengths)
4 1" cubes soft bean curd
2 tbsp ear mushrooms (soaked)
1/4 cup diced carrots
2 tbsp green peas
1 tbsp soaked dried lily flowers (cleaned and
knotted)
2 cups vegetable stock
1/4 cup chinese celery (cut to short lengths)
1/4 cup diced gluten (see page 214)
1 tsp ground pepper
1/2 tsp salt
1 tbsp soy sauce
1 tbsp sugar
fried chopped garlic for garnish

### PREPARATION:
In a medium pot, add vegetable stock
and bring to boil.

Add salted radish, diced carrots, dried lily
flowers, gluten, ear mushrooms, soft bean curd,
mung bean noodles and green peas.

Bring to a boil for 2 mins. Season with pepper,
salt, soy sauce and sugar. Add chinese celery and
remove from stove.

Serve soup in a serving bowl garnished with
chopped fried garlic.

### SERVES 4.

# KHANOM JEEB JEA
## VEGETARIAN STEAMED DUMPLINGS

### INGREDIENTS:
30 sheets of wonton skins
(trim edges to make round)
1/4 cup chopped whole kernel corn
1/4 cup chopped water chestnuts
1/2 cup mashed potatoes
1/4 cup soaked white fungus (cut to florets)
1/4 cup soaked dried shiitake mushrooms
(chopped)
1/4 cup chopped gluten (see page 214)
2 tbsp chopped onions
1 tbsp corn flour
1 tbsp Maggi sauce
1 tbsp sesame oil
1/2 tsp salt
2 tsp ground pepper
1 tbsp sugar
fried chopped garlic, shredded chilli strips,
cilantro leaves and green peas for garnish.

### PREPARATION:
In a mixing bowl, mix corn, water chestnuts,
mashed potatoes, white fungus, chopped shiitake
mushrooms, chopped gluten
and sliced onions together.

Season with Maggi sauce, sesame oil, salt,
ground pepper, sugar and corn flour. Mix well.

Press 1 tbsp filling onto centre of 1 wonton
skin. Place filled wonton into a
greased 1" porcelain cup.

Garnish each filled won ton with green peas,
coriander leaves and red chilli strips.
Steam over high heat for 10 mins.

Remove from cups and serve with chopped fried
garlic and black vinegar sauce.

### SERVES 8.

# HOO CHALAM JEA
## VEGETARIAN SHARK FIN SOUP

### INGREDIENTS:
1/4 cup soaked mung bean noodles
(cut to 2" lengths)
5 soaked dried shiitake mushrooms (sliced)
2 ozs bean sprouts (clean and remove roots)
1/4 cup soaked white fungus (cut to florets)
1/4 cup diced carrots
2 3" coriander roots
3 cups vegetable stock
1/2 tsp ground pepper
1 tsp black soy sauce
2 tbsp soy sauce
2 tbsp Maggi sauce
1/2 tsp salt
1 tbsp sugar
1 tbsp corn flour diluted with 1 tbsp water
red chilli (de-seed and shred for garnish)
chopped spring onion for garnish

### PREPARATION:
In a small pot, add vegetable stock,
coriander roots, sliced shiitake mushrooms,
carrots and white fungus.
Bring to boil over moderate heat for 2 mins.

Season with ground pepper, black soy sauce,
soy sauce, Maggi sauce, salt,
sugar and corn flour mixture.
Boil till mixture thickens.
Add in mung bean noodles and bean sprouts.
Boil till mung bean noodles soften.
Remove from stove.

Serve shark fin soup in a soup bowl
garnished with spring
onion and chilli shreds.

### SERVES 4.

# THOD MAN KHAO PHOD
## CORN FRITTERS

### INGREDIENTS:
1 cup dry bread crumbs
20 sandwich bread slices
2 eggs
2 cups chopped whole kernel corn
1 tsp salt
1 tsp ground pepper
1 tsp sugar
2 tbsp wheat flour
1 tbsp corn flour
2 tbsp vegetable oil
vegetable oil for deep-frying

### PREPARATION:
Cut bread slices into circles with a
3" round cutter.

In a mixing bowl, beat eggs, salt,
ground pepper, sugar and 2 tbsp vegetable oil.
Mix well.

Mix in wheat flour, corn flour and
chopped corn.

With a small palette knife, spread round bread
slices with corn mixture and
coat top with bread crumbs.

Half fill a wok with vegetable oil and
deep-fry thod man in moderately hot oil till
golden and crisp.

Remove and serve corn fritters with
vegetable relish and sauce (see pg 21).

### SERVES 6.

49

# KAENG PHED MA-KHEUA YAO
## EGG PLANT CURRY

### INGREDIENTS:
### CURRY PASTE
8 pepper corns
7 dried chillies (soaked)
1 tsp salt
1 tbsp shredded lemon grass
1 tsp sliced galangal
1/2 tsp rind of kaffir lime
1 tsp sliced fresh turmeric root
1/4 tsp ground nutmeg

### PREPARATION:
In a mortar, grind the above ingredients to a fine paste. Set aside for later use.

### OTHER INGREDIENTS:
4 cups coconut milk
2 tbsp vegetable oil
1/4 cup diced gluten (see page 214)
1/4 cup diced cooked potatoes
1/4 cup diced pineapple
1/4 cup diced baby corn
1/4 cup sliced onions
1 cup green egg plant, cut and soaked
2 tomatoes (cut into wedges)
3 tbsp soy sauce
1 tsp salt
2 tbsp roasted ground sesame seeds
2 tbsp palm sugar
red, green and yellow chillies
(de-seed and slice)

### PREPARATION:
In a frying pan with 2 tbsp vegetable oil, fry the curry paste over low heat till fragrant.

Add in gluten, diced potatoes, pineapple, onions, baby corn and egg plant. Fry till curry paste coats vegetables evenly. Add coconut milk and bring curry to boil for 5 mins.

Add in tomatoes and season with soy sauce, salt and palm sugar. Lastly add in ground sesame seeds and remove from stove.
Garnish with sliced chillies.

**SERVES 4.**

# PHAD PHED MA-KHEUA
## FRIED SPICY EGG PLANT

### INGREDIENTS:
8 oz purple egg plant
1/4 cup sliced baby corn
1/4 cup diced bell peppers
1/4 cup sliced onions
1 tbsp fermented salted beans
1/2 tsp salt
1 tbsp sugar
2 tsp Maggi sauce
1 tbsp chopped garlic
3 tbsp vegetable oil
2 red chillies (de-seed and slice)
sweet basil leaves (horapha) for garnish

### PREPARATION:
Cut egg plant into pieces and soak in cold water for 1/2 hr.

In a frying pan, fry garlic in oil with fermented salted beans for 30 secs.

Drain egg plant and add to frying pan. Add in baby corn, bell pepper, sliced onions and chillies. Stir fry for 2 mins or till egg plant is cooked.

Season with salt, soy sauce, sugar and Maggi sauce. Top with sweet basil leaves and remove from stove.

**SERVES 4.**

# LON HED TAUHOO
## MUSHROOM SAUCE WITH TAMARIND

### INGREDIENTS:
1 cup soft bean curd (mashed)
1/2 cup chopped tomatoes
1/4 cup sliced champignon mushrooms
1/4 cup diced gluten (see page 214)
1/2 cup sliced shallots
1/4 cup palm sugar
2 tsp salt
1/4 cup tamarind juice
2 cups coconut milk
red, green and yellow chillies
(de-seed and slice diagonally)

### PREPARATION:
In a pot, add coconut milk and bring
to boil for 10 mins.

Add in soft bean curd, chopped tomatoes, sliced
mushrooms, diced gluten and sliced shallots.
Lower heat and let simmer for 15 mins.

Season with palm sugar, salt and tamarind juice.
Add sliced chillies.
Remove from stove.

Serve mushroom sauce as a dip with fresh
vegetables.

### SERVES 4.

# PHAK MUAN
## VEGETARIAN CABBAGE ROLLS

### INGREDIENTS:
15 cabbage leaves
1/4 cup sliced fresh mushrooms
1/2 cup soaked mung bean noodles (cut to 2" lengths)
1/4 cup soaked ear mushrooms (shredded)
1/4 cup cooked carrot strips
1/4 cup bean sprouts (clean and remove roots)
1/4 cup cooked red kidney beans
1/4 cup cucumber strips of 1" length
1/4 cup firm white bean curd of 1" strips
1/4 cup bell pepper strips
1 tsp sesame oil
2 tsp sugar
1/2 tsp ground pepper
2 tsp rice vinegar

### PREPARATION:
Bring a pot of water with 1 tsp salt to boil.
Immerse cabbage leaves and let cook in boiling water
for 1 min. Remove with perforated spoon.

Immerse mung bean noodles, fresh mushrooms,
ear mushrooms and bean sprouts in boiling water
for 1 min each and immediately
remove from boiling water with a perforated spoon.
Place mixture in a mixing bowl.

Mix cooked vegetables with carrots, kidney beans,
cucumber, bean curd and bell peppers. Mix well.

Season with sesame oil, sugar, ground pepper and
vinegar. Toss well.

Place 2 tbsp vegetable mixture onto a piece of cabbage
leave. Fold both corners and roll into a cylinder.

Cut cabbage roll into pieces and
arrange on a serving plate.

### SWEET SAUCE
### INGREDIENTS:
1/4 cup soy sauce
1/4 cup palm sugar
2 tsp sesame oil
1 tbsp rice vinegar
1/2 tsp salt
2 tbsp ground roasted sesame seeds

### PREPARATION:
In a small pot, mix ingredients in sauce and bring to
boil. Mix in sesame seeds and remove from stove.
Pour sauce over cabbage rolls.
### SERVES 6.

THE VEGETARIAN TASTE
OF THAILAND

# SALAT MANGSAWIRAT
## VEGETARIAN SALAD

### INGREDIENTS:
1/4  cup fried gluten (see page 214)
1  cup shredded ice-berg lettuce
1/2  cup baby lettuce, shredded
1/4  cup sliced cucumber
1/4  cup sliced tomatoes
2  sliced hard boiled eggs
1/4  cup diced cooked potatoes
1/4  cup diced bell peppers
4  tbsp green peas
1/4  cup cooked kidney beans
1/4  cup whole kernel corn
1/4  cup diced champignon mushrooms

### PREPARATION:
Mix the above ingredients in
a salad bowl and refrigerate.

### PEANUT SAUCE
### INGREDIENTS:
1  cup chucky peanut butter
2  tsp dry chillies (ground)
1/4  cup tamarind juice
1/4  cup plam sugar (chopped)
1/2  tsp salt
2  tbsp vegetable oil
1/2  cup evaporated milk
2  tbsp fried shallots for garnish

### PREPARATION:
In a frying pan, fry ground chillies in
vegetable oil. Add chucky peanut butter and
evaporated milk and let mixture boil.

Add tamarind juice and season with
palm sugar and salt. Remove from stove
and cool mixture before serving with salad.

Pour sauce over vegetables and toss well.
Serve garnished with fried shallots.

### SERVES 4.

# KHAO LAD NAR MANGSAWIRAT
## VEGETARIAN RICE LAD NAR

### INGREDIENTS:
2  cups cooked rice
1/4  cup bamboo shoots cut to 1" strips
3  fresh mushrooms (cut into pieces)
1  tbsp soaked ear mushrooms (shredded)
3  champignon mushrooms (sliced)
2  tbsp green peas
2  tbsp diced gluten (see page 214)
2  tbsp diced tomatoes
2  tbsp diced firm bean curd
1/4  cup sliced abalone mushrooms
4  pitted olives
1  tbsp chopped garlic
2  cups vegetable stock
2  tbsp vegetable oil
2  tbsp corn flour diluted with 1 tbsp water
2  tbsp Maggi sauce
2  tsp sugar
2  tbsp soy sauce
1/2  tsp ground pepper
1  tsp prepared mustard for garnish
sliced spring onion for garnish

### PREPARATION:
Arrange cooked rice on a serving plate.

Fry chopped garlic with oil in
a frying pan till golden.

Add bamboo shoots, all mushrooms, green peas,
tomatoes, bean curd, and olives.
Stir-fry over high heat for about 1 min.

Add stock and season with Maggi sauce, sugar,
soy sauce, ground pepper and corn flour mixture.
Cook till mixture thickens.

Remove from stove and pour over rice.
Garnish with spring onions and mustard.
Serve rice with  pickled chillies.

### SERVES 2.

# KUAI TIAO PHAT THAI
## RICE NOODLE PHAT THAI

### INGREDIENTS:
1 cup rice noodles
1 egg
1 tbsp yellow firm bean curd (diced)
2 tbsp green peas
2 tbsp red kidney beans
1 tbsp minced preserved radish
3 tbsp roasted ground peanuts
2 tbsp sliced shallots
3 tbsp vegetable oil
2 tbsp sugar
2 tbsp soy sauce
3 tbsp tamarind juice
1/4 cup coconut milk
bean sprouts, banana blossoms, lime slices,
chinese chives and carrot shreds for garnish.

### PREPARATION:
In a wok, fry shallots with vegetable oil till
slightly brown and fragrant.

Add radish and break in egg. Fry till egg is
cooked. Add noodles, green peas, red kidney
beans and coconut milk.

Add diced bean curd and ground peanuts.
Season with sugar, soy sauce and tamarind juice.
Toss well and remove from stove.

Serve noodles on a serving plate with fresh
garnish vegetables as above.

### SERVES 2.

# MA-KHEUA PHAO PHAD SAM ROD
## SMOKED EGG PLANT WITH 3 FLAVOURS

### INGREDIENTS:
8 ozs green egg plant (grill and wash to remove
black skin)
2 ozs carrot strips of 1 1/2" lengths
1/4 cup sliced gluten (see page 214)
1/4 cup diced firm white bean curd
1/4 cup roasted cashew nuts
1 sliced hard boiled egg
mint leaves for garnish

### PREPARATION:
Cut grilled egg plant into 1" pieces and
arrange on a serving plate.

Arrange sliced boiled eggs, gluten,
bean curd, carrots and cashew nuts.

Top with sauce and garnish with mint leaves.

### SAUCE
### INGREDIENTS:
1 tbsp hot chillies
3 tbsp lime juice
1 tbsp soy sauce
1/2 tsp salt
2 tbsp sugar

### PREPARATION:
Mix sauce ingredients in a food processor
and blend till well mixed.
Pour sauce over smoked egg plants and serve.

### SERVES 4.

# SUKIYAKI
## VEGETARIAN HOT POT

### INGREDIENTS:
1/2 cup cooked Japanese rice noodles
1/4 cup diced firm white bean curd
2 soaked and sliced ear mushrooms
5 fresh mushrooms (sliced)
1/4 cup Japanese golden mushrooms (enoki)
1/4 cup whole canned champignon mushrooms
1/4 cup baby corn (sliced diagonally)
1/4 cup sliced celery
3 cups vegetable stock

### PREPARATION:
Arrange cooked Japanese rice noodles in a
serving bowl.

In a medium pot, bring vegetable stock to boil.
Add in diced carrots, bean curd,
ear mushrooms, fresh mushrooms, baby corn,
celery, whole champignons and
lastly golden mushrooms (enoki).

Bring soup to boil again and pour over noodles.
Serve with sauce.

### SAUCE
### INGREDIENTS:
2 tbsp fermented red beancurd
1/4 cup sweet chilli sauce
1 tbsp smashed hot chillies
2 tbsp chopped pickled garlic
2 tbsp sesame oil
1 tbsp roasted sesame seeds
2 tbsp rice vinegar
2 tbsp lime juice
3 tbsp sugar
1 tbsp chopped cilantro

### PREPARATION:
Mix all the above ingredients together,
except chopped cilantro, in a blender.
Blend until mixture is smooth.

Top with cilantro and serve with sukiyaki.

### SERVES 1.

# KUAI TIAO SAO NAM
## RICE NOODLES IN COCONUT SAUCE

### INGREDIENTS:
1 cup diced gluten
2 cups cooked Japanese rice noodles
2 cups coconut milk
1/2 cup soft white bean curd chucks
1 tbsp sugar
1 tsp salt
1 tbsp sliced garlic
1 tbsp ginger strips
3 red, green and yellow chillies
(de-seed and slice)
1/4 cup carrot strips of 1" length
1/4 cup pineapple strips of 1" length
lime wedges

### PREPARATION:
In a small pot add coconut milk, diced gluten and
bean curd chucks. Bring to boil.
Season with salt and sugar
and remove from stove.

On a serving plate, arrange rice noodles with
pineapple, carrot and ginger strips, sliced garlic,
sliced chilles and lime wedges.
Serve with hot coconut sauce.

### SERVES 4.

## TOM SOM TAUHOO
### SPICY BEAN CURD SOUP

**INGREDIENTS:**
2 cakes firm white bean curd, cut into 1" pieces
1/4 cup sliced fresh mushrooms
1/4 cup baby corn (cut to 1/2" pieces)
1/2 cup asparagus (cut to 1/2" pieces)
1 tbsp chopped coriander root
1 tsp pepper corns
2 tbsp sliced shallots
3 cups vegetable stock
1 tsp salt
2 tbsp soy sauce
2 tbsp palm sugar
4 tbsp tamarind juice
1 tbsp fried shallots
1 tbsp red chillie shreds
1 tbsp chopped spring onion
2 tbsp ginger shreds

**PREPARATION:**
In a mortar, pound shallots, coriander root and
pepper to a fine paste.

In a medium size pot mix vegetable stock with
the ground paste and bring to boil.

When soup boils, add in bean curd, mushrooms,
corn and asparagus and bring to a full boil.

Season with salt, soy sauce, palm sugar, and
tamarind juice. Simmer for another 15 mins and
remove from stove.

Pour soup into a bowl.
Garnish with fried shallots, spring onions,
chilli shreds and ginger shreds.

**SERVES 4.**

## YAM ASPARAGUS
### SPICY ASPARAGUS SALAD

**INGREDIENTS:**
1 cup asparagus (cut to 1/2" stalks)
1/2 cup diced carrots
1 tbsp hot chillies (smashed)
1/4 cup green peas
2 tbsp roasted chilli paste (nam phrik phao)
1/4 cup lime juice
1/2 tsp soy sauce
2 tsp sugar
1 tbsp fried shallots
1 hard boiled egg (sliced)
mint leaves and red chilli shreds for garnish

**PREPARATION:**
Half fill a medium size pot with water
and bring to boil.

With a perforated spoon, lower asparagus,
carrots and green peas into boiling water
and cook for 2 mins.
Drain and place vegetables in a mixing bowl.
Toss well.

In a small bowl, mix roasted chilli paste,
lime juice, soy sauce and sugar till well mixed.
Mix sauce with vegetables and
toss with fried shallots.

Arrange vegetable salad on a serving plate and
garnish with sliced egg, mint leaves
and chilli shreds.

**SERVES 2.**

# KAPOK PHRA NAM DAENG JEA
## VEGETARIAN FISH MAW SOUP

### INGREDIENTS:
10 crisp gluten balls
1/2 cup baby corn (sliced diagonally)
5 soaked dried shiitake mushrooms (sliced)
1/4 cup white fungus (soaked and cut to florets)
1 tbsp black soy sauce
1 tbsp soy sauce
1 tbsp Maggi sauce
1 tbsp sugar
4 cups mushroom stock
1/4 cup corn flour
1/4 cup vegetable stock
garnish with cilantro sprigs and chilli shreds

### PREPARATION:
In a small bowl, mix corn flour with with 1 cup
of mushroom stock.

In a medium pot, bring remaining stock to boil.
Add in gluten balls, baby corn, mushrooms, and
white fungus and boil for 5 mins.

Season with black soy sauce, soy sauce,
Maggi sauce and sugar.
Thicken with corn flour mixture.
Remove from stove once
soup boils and thickens.

Serve in a serving bowl garnished with coriander
sprigs and chilli shreds.

### SERVES 4.

# PHAT KEP MU TIAM
## CRISPY FRIED MOCK PORK SKIN

### INGREDIENTS:
2 cups gluten (cut into pieces)
1/4 cup red curry paste
4 tbsp vegetable oil
2 tbsp soy sauce
4 tbsp palm sugar
1/2 tsp salt
chilli shreds and kaffir lime leaf shreds
for garnish
vegetable oil for deep frying

### PREPARATION:
In a wok, fill vegetable oil till half full.
Deep fry gluten pieces over moderate heat
till golden and crisp.
Drain.

Remove vegetable oil from wok, retaining 4
tbsp. Fry curry paste over low heat till fragrant.
Add palm sugar, soy sauce and salt.
Mix well till mixture thickens.
Add fried gluten and toss till well mixed.

Remove from stove.
Garnish with chilli and kaffir lime leaf shreds.
Serve hot.

### SERVES 4.

# YAKISOBA
## FRIED EGG NOODLES WITH VEGETABLES

### INGREDIENTS:
1 cup fresh egg noodles
1/4 cup baby corn (sliced diagonally)
2 tbsp soaked ear mushroom shreds
1/4 cup soaked shiitake mushrooms (sliced)
1/4 cup 2" carrot strips
1/4 cup cabbage (cut into pieces)
1 cake firm white bean curd (cut to 1" strips)
2 tbsp green peas
2 tbsp chopped shallots
3 tbsp vegetable oil
2 tsp sesame oil
1 tbsp Maggi sauce
1 tbsp sugar
1 tsp ground pepper
2 tsp soy sauce

### PREPARATION:
In a wok, fry chopped shallots
in vegetable oil till fragrant.

Mix in egg noodles and fry over
high heat for 1 min.

Add baby corn, ear mushrooms, shiitake
mushrooms, carrot strips, cabbage, bean curd and
green peas. Stir fry for another 2 mins.
Season with Maggi sauce, sesame oil, sugar,
ground pepper and soy sauce.

Remove from stove and serve noodles on a
serving platter with pickled chillies.

### SERVES 2.

# SAI LOONG
## RAINBOW NOODLES

### INGREDIENTS:
1 cup soaked mungbean noodles
(cut to 2" lengths)
1/4 cup 2" carrot strips
1/4 cup chinese celery (cut to 1" lengths)
1/4 cup tomato wedges
1/4 cup firm white bean curd cut to 1" strips
1/4 cup roasted ground peanuts
1 tbsp fried chopped garlic
1 tbsp hot chillies (smashed)
2 tbsp soy sauce
4 tbsp lime juice
1/2 tsp salt
1 tsp sugar
lettuce and cilantro sprigs for garnish

### PREPARATION:
In a medium pot, half fill with water and
bring to boil. Immerse mungbean noodles on a
perforated spoon to cook. When mungbean
noodles turn soft, drain and place in
a mixing bowl.

Mix mungbean noodles with carrot strips,
celery, tomato wedges, bean curd strips,
ground peanuts and fried garlic.
Toss mixture well.
Serve on a serving plate arranged with
lettuce and garnish with cilantro sprigs.

### SERVES 4.

# KHANOM HUA PHAK KAT
### RADISH CAKE

### INGREDIENTS:
1 1/2  cups grated chinese white radish
1 1/2  cups grated carrots
3  cups rice flour
1  tbsp corn flour
2  tsp salt
2  tsp ground pepper
3  tbsp chopped preserved radish
6  cups vegetable stock

### PREPARATION:
Cook the above together in a pot till thick.

Pour mixture into an oiled 10" x 10" x 2" square
baking tray and steam over high heat for
1 hr. or until a skewer inserted comes out clean.
Cool cake and cut into 1" squares.

### FRIED RADISH CAKE
### INGREDIENTS:
1 1/2  cups steamed 1" square radish cakes
3  soaked dried shiitake mushrooms (sliced)
1/4  cup ear mushroom shreds
1/4  cup chinese celery (cut to 1" lengths)
1/2  cup cleaned bean sprouts without roots
2  tbsp chopped garlic
1  tbsp chopped preserved radish
3  tbsp vegetable oil
1  tbsp soy sauce
1  tbsp Maggi sauce
1  tbsp sugar
1  tsp ground black pepper

### PREPARATION:
In a wok, fry chopped garlic and preserved
radish in oil till garlic turns golden. Add in radish
cakes and fry till crisp.

Season with soy sauce, Maggi sauce, sugar and
ground black pepper.

Toss in bean sprouts and celery and stir fry over
high heat till cooked, about 2 mins.

Remove from stove and serve on a platter with
more fresh vegetables and pickled chillies.

### SERVES 2.

# PHAK PRIEW WAN
### SWEET AND SOUR VEGETABLES

### INGREDIENTS:
1/4  cup lychees in syrup (drain and cut in half)
1/4  cup celery (sliced diagonally)
1/4  cup bell pepper strips of 1" length
1/4  cup sliced fresh mushrooms
1/4  cup diced pineapple
5  1" x 1" cubes of firm white bean curd
1/4  cup diced cooked potatoes
1/4  cup sliced tomato wedges
1/2  tsp ground black pepper
4  tbsp tomato sauce
1  tbsp chilli sauce
2  tbsp sugar
2  tbsp rice vinegar
1/2  tsp salt
4  tbsp cornflour
2  cups vegetable stock
1  tbsp chopped garlic
2  cups soaked rice vermicelli
vegetable oil for deep-frying

### PREPARATION:
Prepare vegetable oil for deep-frying.

Toss drained rice vermicelli into moderately hot
oil and fry till vermicelli turns golden and crisp.
Remove with perforated spoon and drain.

Arrange crisp vermicelli on a serving plate.

Drain wok and replace with 2 tbsp oil.
Fry chopped garlic till golden.
Add in lychees, celery, bell pepper,
mushrooms, diced pineapple, bean curd,
potatoes, tomatoes and 1 cup vegetable stock.
Boil for 5 mins.

To the remaining stock, stir in corn flour.
Mix in ground pepper, tomato sauce,
chilli sauce, sugar, vinegar and salt.
Pour mixture into boiling sauce and
boil till sauce thickens.
Remove from stove and pour sweet and sour
sauce over crisp vermicelli.

### SERVES 4.

# MACARONI
## PHAT KEE MAO
### SPICY FRIED MACARONI

### INGREDIENTS:
1 cup cooked macaroni(or any pasta)
1/4 cup straw mushrooms (cut to halves)
1/4 cup sliced onions
1/2 cup broccoli (cut to florets)
1 cake firm bean curd (sliced lengthwise and cut into strips)
1/4 cup tomato wedges
1 red chilli (de-seed and slice diagonally)
1 tbsp hot chillies, smashed
2 tbsp vegetable oil
1 tbsp chopped garlic
1 egg
1 tbsp Maggi sauce
1 tbsp soy sauce
1 tbsp sugar
deep-fried basil leaves (kapao) for garnishing

### PREPARATION:
In a wok, with vegetable oil, fry chopped garlic till golden. Add in pasta, straw mushrooms, sliced onions, broccoli, bean curd strips, tomato wedges, sliced chillies and smashed hot chillies.

Stir-fry till cooked, about 3 mins.
Stir in egg and fry till well mixed.
Season with Maggi sauce, soy sauce and sugar.

Remove from stove and serve on a platter garnished with deep-fried basil leaves.

### SERVES 2.

# YUM HED KROP
### SPICY CRUNCHY MUSHROOM SALAD

### INGREDIENTS:
1 cup fresh mushrooms (halved)
1/4 cup 2" carrot strips
1/4 cup cilantro (cut to 1" lengths)
1/4 cup bell pepper (cut to 1" strips)
iceberg lettuce for garnish

### PREPARATION:
Arrange cleaned iceberg lettuce on a serving plate.

Mix mushrooms, carrots, cilantro and bell peppers in a mixing bowl.
Add sauce and toss vegetables well.
Arrange vegetables over lettuce on the serving plate.

### SAUCE
### INGREDIENTS:
2 tsp chopped garlic
4 tbsp lime juice
2 tbsp soy sauce
1/2 tsp salt
2 tbsp sugar
1 tbsp hot chillies ( ground)
3 tbsp peanut butter

### PREPARATION:
In a small mixing bowl, mix the sauce ingredients together.
Use as required.

### SERVES 4.

# ROM SAR HAI
## STEWED VEGETABLES

### INGREDIENTS:
1/2  cup soaked mung bean noodles
(cut to 2" lengths)
1/2  cup chinese mustard (cut to 2" lengths)
1/2  cup chinese celery (cut to 1" lengths)
5  fresh mushrooms (sliced)
1/4  cup soaked lily flowers
5  2" soft bean curd squares
1/4  cup soaked white fungus (cut to florets)
4  tbsp vegetable oil
1  tbsp chopped garlic
1  tbsp soy sauce
2  tbsp Maggi sauce
1  tbsp sugar
1/4  tsp salt
1/2  cup vegetable stock
1  tbsp corn flour diluted with 1 tbsp water
"roast pork" gluten, sliced
(available in vegetarian stores)

### PREPARATION:
Half fill a medium pot with water
and bring to boil.

With a perforated spoon, immerse mung bean
noodles to cook till soft.
Drain and arrange on a serving plate.

Cook chinese mustard, sliced mushrooms, lily
flowers, bean curd and white fungus in boiling
water for 1 min and drain with perforated spoon.
Arrange celery and cooked vegetables
on a serving plate with mung bean noodles .

In a frying pan, fry garlic with vegetable oil till
golden. Add vegetable stock and season with
soy sauce, Maggi sauce, sugar and salt.
Thicken with corn flour mixture and
bring sauce to boil till thick.
Remove from stove and pour over mungbean
noodles and vegetables.
Garnish with roasted pork gluten slices.
Serve hot.

### SERVES 2.

# KIOW MANGSAWIRAT
## VEGETARIAN WONTON SOUP

### INGREDIENTS:
20  wonton skins
1/2  cup spinach (shred finely)
1/2  cup cooked Japanese rice noodles
1/4  cup finely diced gluten (see page 214)
1/4  cup minced firm white bean curd
1/4  cup finely diced carrots
1/4  cup sliced fresh mushrooms
2  tbsp vegetable oil
1  tbsp chopped shallots
1  tbsp Maggi sauce
1  tsp ground pepper
2  tsp sugar
1/2  tsp salt
1  tsp sesame oil

### PREPARATION:
In a frying pan with vegetable oil
fry chopped onions till golden.
Add gluten, carrots, mushrooms and spinach.

Over high heat, stir-fry for 2 mins then add minced
bean curd. Season with ground pepper, Maggi sauce,
sugar, salt and sesame oil. Fry till well mixed.
Cool and use for filling.

Place 1 tbsp filling on wonton skin and seal edges
with water. Bind wonton with rice noodles
and secure with a knot.

Drop wantons into hot soup to cook.

### SOUP
### INGREDIENTS:
1/4  cup carrot strips of 1" lengths
1  tbsp ginger shreds
2  cups vegetable stock
1  tbsp Maggi sauce
1  tbsp soy sauce
1  tsp ground pepper
1  tsp sugar
fried garlic for garnish

### PREPARATION:
In a medium pot, bring vegetable stock to boil. Add in
carrot strips and ginger shreds. Season with soy sauce,
Magi sauce and ground pepper.

Bring soup to boil and add wonton. When wonton
floats, remove pot from stove. Laddle wonton soup
into a serving bowl and  garnish with fried garlic.
Serve hot.

### SERVES 4.

# YAM LABB HED CHAMPIGNON
## SPICY MIXED MUSHROOM SALAD

### INGREDIENTS:
1/2 cup diced champignon mushrooms
1/4 cup ear mushrooms (soaked and sliced)
1 cake diced firm white bean curd
4 tbsp lime juice
1 tbsp roasted ground rice
1 tsp ground chilli powder
1 tbsp palm sugar
1 tbsp soy sauce
1/4 cup roasted cashew nuts
1 tbsp chopped spring onions
1 tbsp chopped cilantro
2 tbsp sliced shallots
lettuce, mint leaves and chilli shreds for garnish

### PREPARATION:
In a medium pot, 1/2 fill with water and bring to boil. With a perforated spoon, cook mushrooms and bean curd for 1 min each. Drain and place in a mixing bowl.

Mix in lime juice, roasted ground rice, chilli powder, palm sugar and soy sauce. Toss till well mixed.

Add cashew nuts, spring onions, chopped cilantro and sliced shallots. Mix well. Serve on a lettuce lined platter. Garnish with mint leaves and chilli shreds.

### SERVES 2.

# KIOW KROP FRUIT SALAD
## FRIED WONTON WITH FRUIT SALAD

### INGREDIENTS:
30 wonton skins
5 straw mushrooms (sliced)
1/2 cup mashed potatoes
2 tbsp finely diced carrots
2 tbsp finely diced bell pepper
2 tbsp finely diced water chestnuts
2 hard boiled eggs (cut into chucks)
1/4 cup finely diced gluten
1 tbsp Maggi sauce
2 tsp sugar
1 tbsp sesame oil
1 tsp salt
2 tsp ground pepper

### PREPARATION:
Mix sliced straw mushrooms, mashed potatoes, diced carrots, bell peppers, water chestnuts and gluten together in a mixing bowl to form a paste.

Season with Maggi sauce, sugar, sesame oil, salt and pepper.

Place 1 tbsp filling on each wonton skin and top with a chuck of hard boiled egg. Brush edges of wonton skin with water and seal into a triangular shape, securing both ends together.

In a wok, fill with oil for deep-frying and bring to boil. Drop wantons into oil and deep fry till golden and crisp.

Drain and place on a serving plate. Serve with fruit salad.

### SALAD
### INGREDIENTS:
1 cup mayonnaise
1/2 cup fruit cocktail

### PREPARATION:
Mix mayonnaise and fruit cocktail together. Serve with crisp wantons.

### SERVES 4.

## TOM KEM SAI MOO
### VEGETARIAN BLACK SAUCE PORK

### INGREDIENTS:
1 cup spongy fried bean curd squares
1/4 cup diced firm white bean curd
1/2 cup gluten (cut into chucks)
1/4 cup soaked dried shiitake mushrooms
(sliced)
1/4 cup cooked peanuts with skin
2 tbsp chopped coriander roots
2 tbsp sliced garlic
2 tsp pepper corns
2 pieces star anise
3 pieces cinnamon stick of 1" lengths
1/4 cup palm sugar
1 tbsp soy sauce
3 tbsp Maggi sauce
1/4 cup black soy sauce
2 tbsp vegetable oil
8 cups vegetable tock
sprigs of cilantro for garnish

### PREPARATION:
In a mortar mix coriander roots, garlic and
pepper together. Pound till a fine paste.

In a wok, with 2 tbsp vegetable oil, fry the
ground paste till fragrant. Add in 1/2 amount
stock, star anise, cinnamon sticks, palm sugar,
soy sauce, black sauce, Maggi sauce and
bring to boil over high heat.

Transfer mixture into a medium sized pot and
add in remaining stock, spongy bean curd
squares, firm white bean curd, gluten,
sliced shiitake mushrooms, and peanuts.

Simmer over low heat for 1/2 hour. Remove
from stove and serve in a serving bowl
with cilantro sprigs.

### SERVES 4.

## MACARONI NAM
### MACARONI SOUP

### INGREDIENTS:
1 cup cooked macaroni
1/4 cup ear mushrooms (soaked and sliced)
5 soaked dried shiitake mushrooms (sliced)
1/4 cup deep-fried spongy bean curd squares
(cut into strips)
1/4 cup spiced gluten (from Tom Kem Sai Moo)
1/4 cup diced tomatoes
1/4 cup chinese celery (cut to 1" lengths)
1/4 cup fresh mushrooms (halved)
4 cups vegetable stock
1/2 tsp salt
2 tsp soy sauce
2 tsp Maggi sauce
1 tsp ground pepper
1 tsp sesame oil

### PREPARATION:
In a medium pot, bring vegetable stock to boil
and add cooked macaroni, mushrooms, spongy
bean curd squares, and spiced gluten.

Let soup boil for 5 mins. Add in tomatoes and
celery. Bring to boil again for another 2 mins
over high heat and season with salt, soy sauce,
Maggi sauce, ground pepper and sesame oil.
Remove from stove and serve immediately.

### SERVES 2.

# KAENG SOM PHAK RUAM
## SPICY MIXED VEGETARIAN SOUP

### INGREDIENTS:
### RED CHILLI PASTE
1/4 cup dried chillies (soaked and cut in pieces)
1/2 tsp salt
1/4 cup shallots
2 tbsp garlic

### PREPARATION:
In a mortar, pound dried chillies, salt, shallots
and garlic to a fine paste.

### OTHER INGREDIENTS:
1/2 cup diced baby corn
1/4 cup diced mushrooms
1/2 cup asparagus (cut to 1" lengths)
1/2 cup sliced carrots
1/2 cup white chinese cabbage (cut to 1" pieces)
1/2 cup broccoli (cut to florets)
4 cups vegetable stock
1/2 tsp salt
3 tbsp soy sauce
3 tbsp plam sugar
1/4 cup tamarind juice

### PREPARATION:
In a medium pot, fill with vegetable stock and
bring to boil. Add in chilli paste and season with
salt, soy sauce, palm sugar,
and tamarind juice.

Add in diced baby corn, mushrooms,
asparagus, sliced carrots,
white cabbage and broccoli.
Bring to boil again, remove
from stove and serve.

### SERVES 4.

# PHAK CHUP PHANG THOD
## VEGETABLE FRITTERS

### INGREDIENTS:
1/2 cup carrots (cut to 2" x 1" sticks)
1/2 cup baby corn (cut to 2" pieces)
1/2 cup asparagus (cut to 2" stalk)
1/2 cup raw papaya (cut to 2" x 1/2" sticks)

### BATTER
### INGREDIENTS:
1 cup rice flour
1/2 cup wheat flour
1 tsp baking powder
1 tbsp chopped onions
2 tbsp roasted ground peanuts
2 tsp sugar
1 3/4 cups water
1/4 tsp salt

### PREPARATION:
In a mixing bowl, sift rice flour, wheat flour and
baking powder together. Add in salt, sugar and
slowly mix with water till batter is smooth.

Add in ground nuts and chopped onions.
Rest batter for 15 mins before use
Half fill a wok with vegetable oil.
Dip vegetables into batter and deep fry in
moderately hot oil till golden and crisp.

Arrange on a serving plate
to be served with sauce.

### SAUCE
### INGREDIENTS:
2 cups tamarind juice
1/2 cup palm sugar
1 tsp salt
1 cup sugar
2 tbsp red chillies (ground)
cilantro sprigs and roasted chopped
peanuts for garnish

### PREPARATION:
In a small pot, mix tamarind juice, palm sugar,
salt, sugar and ground chillies. Bring to boil.

Cook mixture till thick and remove from
stove. Garnish with
roasted chopped peanuts and cilantro sprigs.

### SERVES 4.

# KAENG JEUD TANG KWA
## CLEAR CUCUMBER SOUP

### INGREDIENTS:
8 ozs cucumber carved with leaf designs
1/4 cup sliced gluten
1/4 cup soaked dried shiitake mushrooms
(sliced)
1/4 cup diced fresh mushrooms
3 cups mushroom stock
1 tbsp Maggi sauce
2 tsp sugar
1 tsp sesame oil
1/2 tsp salt
chopped spring onions for garnish

### PREPARATION:
Fill a medium size pot with mushroom stock and
bring to boil. Add in sliced gluten, mushrooms
and season with Maggi sauce, soy sauce, sugar,
sesame oil and salt.

Add in cucumber pieces and cook for 5
mins. Remove from stove and serve soup in a
serving bowl garnished with spring onion.

### SERVES 4.

# KHAO OP PHUAK
## BAKED TARO ROOT RICE

### INGREDIENTS:
1 1b taro root (clean and cut 2" from top,
hollow centre and carve taro root)
2 cups cooked rice
1/2 cup diced taro root (from hollowed taro root)
1/4 cup diced carrots
1/4 cup cooked peanuts with skin
1/4 cup cooked kidney beans
2 tbsp chopped preserved radish
1/4 cup green peas
2 tbsp chopped garlic
1 tbsp Maggi sauce
1 tbsp soy sauce
1 tbsp sugar
1 tsp pepper
1/2 tsp salt
2 tbsp vegetable oil
garnish with roasted cashew nuts, chopped
cilantro and chilli shreds.

### PREPARATION:
In a frying pan with vegetable oil fry garlic till
golden. Add in radish and diced taro root and
stir-fry over high heat for 2 mins. Stir in carrots,
peanuts, kidney beans and green peas.

Add rice, mix well and season with
Maggi sauce, soy sauce, sugar,
salt and pepper.

Spoon rice into hollowed out taro root
and cover with lid.
Steam over high heat for 15 mins.

Remove from steamer and garnish with
cashew nuts, cilantro sprigs
and chilli shreds and serve.

### SERVES 2.

# SEAFOOD

Nowadays seafood is listed as the most popular food among Thai families. Seafood products like fishballs or fishcakes are always found on our everyday menu. Besides its savoury taste, seafood is very nutritious and provides high-quality protein, useful fat, carbohydrates, minerals and vitamins.

Seafood is generally divided into 2 types i.e. fish and shellfish. Various kinds of fish have different levels of fat, those with white meat such as sole or mackerel contain less than 2% Fat. Fish such as cod has around 2-5% fat and darker coloured fish such as salmon, eel or trout contains over 5% fat. There are two types of shellfish: mollusks such as squid or oysters and crustaceans such as shrimp or crab.

Seafood provides high-quality and easily digested protein which is suitable even for small children. The low levels of fat, except for some kinds of seafood such as salmon or oysters, makes it a practical diet-control menu. However, fat from seafood or fish-liver oil provides lots of vitamin A and D. Carbohydrates in seafood are in in the form of glycogen which will, when cooked, become glucose; a single molecule sugar that instantly gives energy to the body.

The most important mineral that seafood provides is iodine which the body needs in order to produce Thyroxin Hormone which controls the body's metabolism. The lack of iodine will result in the overfunctioning of the thyroid gland, normally known as a goitre, a crucial malnutrition disease found mostly in the northern parts of Thailand. Besides iodine, seafood also a provides a source of calcium, phosphorus, iron, copper, vitamin A, D, B1 and B2.

*When buying Seafood, choose only fresh seafood, the following tips may help when shopping:*

**Fish** : Clear eyes, red gills, head and scales adhere to the body, no foul odours

**Shrimp** : Head adheres to the body, no foul odours, blue or greyish shell

**Crab** : Good weight, eyes moving, male will have more meat than female, female with eggs will give a solid sound when the shell is tapped

**Shellfish** : No foul odours, tightly closed or reacts when touched

Eat only well-cooked seafood. Seafood is preferably cooked at high temperatures for a short time i.e. 100 degrees centigrade (*) for 5 minutes or 80 degrees centigrade for 8-10 minutes.

Seafood is gaining more and more popularity in Thailand these days. There are large numbers of seafood outlets from which to choose; from footpath stalls to big name restaurants.

Seafood can be included in almost every recipe, from grilling to boiling or steaming. Or you may like it fried, pan fried or oriental-style deep fried. Thai dishes are perfectly matched with seafood, ranging from a simple dish like fried rice or noodles to a more sophisticated and classic dish like Tom Yam or Tomkha. The most important factor to consider when cooking seafood is freshness.

Dipping or seasoning sauces for seafood may come in a variety of selections. However the main ingredients are garlic, fish sauce or soy sauce, lime juice, sugar and chillies.

* 100 degrees centigrade equals 212 degrees Fahrenheit.

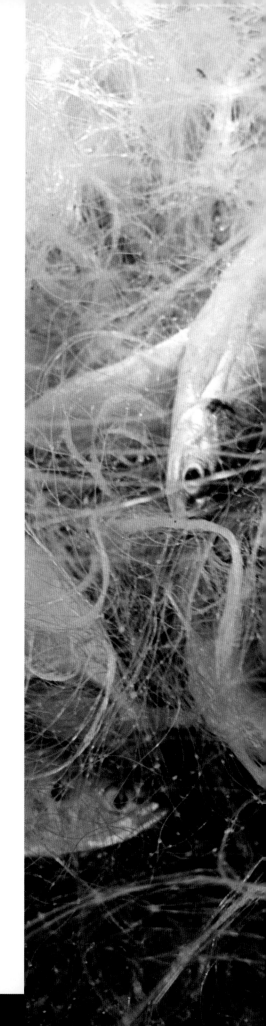

## HO MOK POO
### STEAMED SPICY CRAB
### CUSTARD IN PUMPKIN

**INGREDIENTS:**

One 60 oz carved pumpkin
1 cup steamed crab meat
5 ozs fresh fish, diced
1 egg
1 1/4 cup thick coconut milk
1 tbsp fish sauce
1/4 cup chilli paste
1/4 cup sweet basil leaves (horapha)
1/4 cup carrot strips (1" length)
1/4 cup sliced cooked cabbage
chilli shreds and
kaffir lime leaf shreds for garnish,
thick coconut cream for topping

**PREPARATION:**
Arrange carrot strips and cooked cabbage
inside carved pumpkin.
Mix crab meat, diced fish, egg, chilli paste,
coconut milk and fish sauce together.
Mix well and add basil leaves.
Fill carved pumpkin with this mixture and
steam with lid over high heat for 20 mins.
Remove from steamer.
Remove lid and pour coconut cream over
the top of crab custard.
Garnish with chilli and kaffir lime leaf shreds.

COCONUT CREAM:
Mix 1/2 cup thick coconut milk with
1/2 tsp rice flour in a small pot and
bring to boil till thick.
Use for topping.

**SERVES 4.**

## YAM PLA DOOK FOO
### FLUFFY CAT FISH SALAD
### WITH SOUR MANGO

**INGREDIENTS:**

1 1b  smoked cat fish
1/2  cup unripe mango (remove peel and shred)
1/4  cup carrot strips of 1" length)
1 tbsp shallots (sliced)
2  stalks chinese celery (cut to 1" length)
1/4  cut roasted cashew nuts
mint leaves and chilli shreds for garnish
vegetable oil for deep frying

**PREPARATION:**

Remove flesh from smoked cat fish and chop
meat to a fine paste.

In a wok, fill with oil till 1/2 full and drop
minced fish into  moderately hot oil and stir till
meat spreads out like a net and  turns golden.

Immediately, remove with a perforated spoon
and place fluffy cat fish on a
banana leaf lined serving plate.

Top with mango shreds, carrots,
roasted cashew nuts, sliced shallots and
chinese celery.
Garnish with mint leaves and chilli shreds.
Pour sauce over salad and serve.

**SAUCE**
**INGREDIENTS:**

2  tbsp hot chillies (smashed)
3  tbsp fish sauce
1  tbsp sugar
4  tbsp lime juice

**PREPARATION:**

Mix hot chillies, fish sauce, sugar
and lime juice in a mixing bowl.
Mix till sugar dissolves and serve
over cat fish salad.

**SERVES 4.**

# PLA MEUK KWAY LUI FAI
**SPICY CUTTLEFISH**

### INGREDIENTS:

10 oz  cuttlefish (clean and cut into 1/2" rings)
2 tbsp chopped garlic
2 tbsp chopped shallots
2 tbsp chopped hot chillies
1/2  cup chilli sauce
1/4  cup pineapple juice
1 tbsp sugar
1 tbsp fish sauce
3 tbsp vegetable oil
lettuce leaves and
chilli shreds for garnish

### PREPARATION;

Fill pot with water and bring to a boil.
Add in cuttlefish and cook for 3 minutes,
drain with a perforated spoon.

Place cuttlefish in a mixing bowl.

In a frying pan, fry chopped garlic, shallots and
hot chillies with oil till fragrant. Add in chilli
sauce, pineapple juice and
season with sugar and fish sauce.

Remove sauce once it boils and add
to cuttlefish in mixing bowl.
Mix well.

Line a serving plate with lettuce and
top with spicy cuttlefish.
Garnish with chilli shreds.

**SERVES 4.**

# KAAM POO NENG SEE YU KRA-THIAM
**STEAMED CRAB CLAWS WITH GARLIC & SOY SAUCE**

### INGREDIENTS:

10  sea crab claws
10  cloves peeled garlic (chopped)
2 tbsp chinese wine
1/4  cup soy sauce
1  tbsp oyster sauce
2 tsp prepared mustard
2 tsp sesame oil
cilantro sprigs for garnish

### PREPARATION:

Clean and smash crab claws.
Steam crab claws over high heat
for 10 mins or till cooked.

Remove from steamer and arrange cooked
claws on a serving plate.

In a small mixing bowl, mix chopped garlic,
chinese wine, soy sauce, oyster sauce,
mustard and sesame oil together.

Pour sauce over cooked crab claws
and garnish with cilantro sprigs.

**SERVES 6.**

# KAENG KEOW WAN KUNG FUKTHONG
**GREEN CURRY WITH PUMPKIN AND PRAWNS**

### INGREDIENTS:

1  cup pumpkin cut to 1" x 2" pieces
5  big prawns (cleaned)
3  cups coconut milk
1/4  cup evaporated milk
1  tbsp palm sugar
3  tbsp fish sauce
1/4  cup green curry paste
3  tbsp vegetable oil
2  kaffir lime leaves (torn)
2  red chillies (de-seeded and sliced)
sweet basil leaves (horapha)

### PREPARATION:

In a medium pot, add vegetable oil and
fry green curry paste
over low heat till fragrant.

Add coconut milk and evaporated milk and
bring to boil for 5 mins.

Season with palm sugar and fish sauce.

Add in pumpkin pieces and prawns.
Simmer till cooked.

Drop in kaffir lime leaves, red chillies and
sweet basil leaves and remove from stove.
Serve hot with fried or cooked rice noodles.

**SERVES 4.**

# PLA MEUK YANG KAP SAUCE
**GRILLED SQUID WITH CHILLI SAUCE**

### INGREDIENTS:

10 ozs  squid
(clean, remove membrane and tentacles)
4  tbsp chilli sauce
1  tbsp chopped garlic
1  tsp soy sauce
1  tsp sugar
1  tbsp Maggi sauce
1  tsp ground pepper

### PREPARATION:

Place cleaned squid in mixing bowl.

Mix in chilli sauce, chopped garlic, soy sauce,
sugar, Maggi sauce and ground pepper.
Marinate for 1/2 hour.

Grill marinated squid,
brushing with margarine
till cooked.

Cut squid into pieces and
arrange on a serving plate.
Serve with sauce.

### SAUCE INGREDIENTS:

1/2  cup chilli sauce
1/4  cup mayonnaise

### PREPARATION:

Mix well and serve with grilled squid.

**SERVES 4.**

# HOI MALANG POO
# OP MOR DIN
**BAKED MUSSELS**

### INGREDIENTS:

2  lbs mussels
1/4  cup sliced lemon grass
3  red, green and yellow chillies
(de-seed and slice)
5  kaffir lime leaves (torn)
10  slices galangal
1/4  cup sweet basil leaves (horapha)
15  hot chillies (smashed)
1  cup coconut milk
basil leaves and sliced chillies for garnish

### PREPARATION:

Soak mussels in a pot of water to clean.
Drain and place in a  claypot.

To the mussels, add lemon grass, sliced chillies,
lime leaves, galangal, sweet basil leaves,
hot chillies and coconut milk.

Cover pot and cook over low heat for 15 mins.
Remove from claypot and garnish with more
basil leaves and sliced chillies.
Serve with sauce.

### SAUCE
### INGREDIENTS:

2  tbsp hot chillies (smashed)
1  tbsp chopped coriander root
1  tbsp garlic (sliced)
2  tbsp fish sauce
3  tbsp lime juice
1  tbsp sugar

### PREPARATION:

In a mortar, pound hot chillies, coriander root
and garlic till fine.

Remove and mix in a small bowl with fish
sauce, lime juice and sugar.
Stir well till sugar dissolves and serve with
mussels.

### SERVES 4.

# HOI LAI PHAT
# NAM PHRIK PHAO
**FRIED CLAMS IN ROASTED CHILLI PASTE**

### INGREDIENTS:

1  1b  clams
2  tbsp chopped garlic
1/4  cup bell pepper (sliced diagonally)
1  onion (sliced)
1  tomato (cut into wedges)
1  red chilli (de-seeded and sliced diagonally)
1/4  cup sweet basil leaves (horapha)
2  tsp sugar
1  tbsp fish sauce
1  tbsp hot chillies (smashed)
4  tbsp roasted chilli paste (nam phrik phao)
2  tbsp vegetable oil

### PREPARATION:

Soak clams in a pot of water for 1/2 hour
to remove dirt.

In a wok, with vegetable oil,
fry chopped garlic till golden.
Mix in roasted chilli paste and hot chillies
Add clams and stir-fry over high heat for 1 min.

Season with sugar and fish sauce.
Toss in bell peppers, onions,  tomatoes
and sweet basil leaves.
Stir-fry until clams are cooked and opened.
Immediately remove from stove and serve.

### SERVES 4.

# PLA KAO NENG TAU SEE
### STEAMED GROUPER
### WITH FERMENTED BEANS

## INGREDIENTS:

12  oz  grouper fillet (cut into 2 thick slices)
1/2  tsp salt
1/4  cup fine carrot shreds of 2" length
1/4  cup ginger shreds of 1" length
1/4  cup sliced bacon strips
1  tbsp oyster sauce
2  tbsp Chinese wine
1  tbsp sesame oil
1  tsp sugar
2  tsp Maggi sauce
2  spring onions (cut to 1" lengths)
1  tbsp chopped garlic
2  tbsp fermented black beans
1  chilli (shreded) for garnish

## PREPARATION:

In a mixing bowl rub salt over fish fillets.
Season with oyster sauce, sesame oil, sugar,
Maggi sauce and Chinese wine.

Line a porcelain serving plate with carrot and
ginger shreds. Place fish fillets on top of carrot
and ginger shreds. Top fillets with bacon,
chopped garlic and fermented beans.

Steam over high heat for 10 mins.
Remove from  steamer.
Garnish with chilli shreds and serve.

## SERVES 4.

# PHAT TOM YAM THALAY
### STIR FRIED TOM YAM SEAFOOD

## INGREDIENTS:

1/4  cup squid (cleaned, scored and sliced)
1/2  cup sliced white fish fillets
1/4  cup mussels (cleaned)
1/4  cup prawns (shelled)
3  3" pieces lemon grass (sliced diagonally)
3  kaffir lime leaves (torn)
6  slices galangal
10  hot chillies (smashed)
1  tbsp thick tamarind juice
2  tbsp roasted chilli paste (nam phrik phao)
2  tbsp lime juice
2  tbsp fish sauce
2  tbsp sugar
1  tomato (cut into wedges)
2  tbsp chopped garlic
2  tbsp vegetable oil
1/4  cup evaporated milk
cilantro sprigs for garnish

## PREPARATION:

In a wok with 2 tbsp vegetable oil fry chopped
garlic till golden.

Add in squid, fish fillets, mussels and prawns
and stir fry over  high heat for 30 secs.

Stir-fry mixture till well mixed and season with
thick tamarind juice, lime juice, fish sauce, sugar
and evaporated milk.

Add tomato wedges and fry for another 1 min.
Remove from stove and serve with
cilantro sprigs.

## SERVES 4.

# KAENG SOM POH TAEK
## SOUR SEAFOOD AND VEGETABLE SOUP

### KAENG SOM CHILLI PASTE
### INGREDIENTS:

7 dried chillies (soaked)
4 yellow chillies (cut into pieces)
1/4 cup sliced shallots
2 tbsp sliced garlic
1/2 tsp salt
1 tsp shrimp paste

### PREPARATION:

In a mortar, mix dried chillies, yellow chillies,
shallots, garlic, salt and shrimp paste together.
Pound till mixture resembles a fine paste.

### OTHER INGREDIENTS:

1/4 cup tamarind juice
2 tbsp palm sugar
4 cups chicken stock
3 tbsp fish sauce
1/2 cup sliced carrots
1/2 cup asparagus (cut to 1" stalks)
1/2 cup chinese cabbage (cut to pieces)
1/2 cup sliced white fish fillets
1/4 cup cleaned clams
1 crab (cut into pieces)
1/4 cup prawns (cleaned and shelled)

### PREPARATION:

In a medium pot bring chicken stock to boil.
Mix in ground chilli paste.
Season stock with tamarind juice,
palm sugar and fish sauce.

Add carrots, asparagus and
chinese cabbage and bring to boil.
Lastly, add in sliced fish fillets, clams,
crab and shelled prawns.
Let soup boil again and remove from stove.
Serve hot.

### SERVES 4.

# TOM SOM
# PLA KAPHONG DAENG
## SPICY RED SNAPPER SOUP

### INGREDIENTS:

1 lb red snapper fillets
(cut across grain into thick slices)
1 tbsp chopped shallots
4 3" coriander roots
10 ground pepper corns (smashed)
2 kaffir lime leaves (torn)
2 tbsp hot chillies (smashed)
1/4 cup fine ginger shreds
1/4 cup spring onions (cut to 1" lengths)
2 tbsp fish sauce
1 tbsp palm sugar
1/4 cup tamarind juice
3 cups chicken stock
1 tsp salt

### PREPARATION:

In a mortar pound shallots, coriander roots
and pepper corns to a fine paste.

In a medium pot bring stock to boil and
mix in ground paste.

Add fish slices and simmer over stove
without stirring for 10 mins.

Season with fish sauce, palm sugar,
tamarind juice and salt.

Add kaffir lime leaves, hot chillies,
ginger shreds and spring onions.
Immediately remove from stove and
serve hot.

### SERVES 4.

# THALAY PHA-NAENG SAM ROT
## THREE FLAVOUR SEAFOOD IN RED CURRY SAUCE

### INGREDIENTS:
2  big prawns (clean and leave intact)
8  ozs  cuttlefish
(clean, score and slice into 2" x 4" pieces)
8 ozs  white fish fillets (slice to 1/4" thick pieces)
1/4  cup red curry paste
2  cups coconut milk
1/2  cup roasted ground peanuts
1/4  cup evaporated milk
2  tbsp fish sauce
1  tbsp palm sugar
3  kaffir lime leaves (torn)
chilli shreds and kaffir lime leaf shreds
for garnish
3  tbsp vegetable oil for frying

### PREPARATION:

Half fill wok with vegetable oil.
Straighten and secure prawns with skewers.
Deep fry till cooked, about 3 mins.

Remove skewers from prawns and
arrange on a serving plate.

Deep-fry cuttlefish slices and
fish fillets till cooked.
Drain and arrange on serving plate with prawns.

Remove oil from wok and
replace with 3 tbsp. oil.
Add curry paste and fry till fragrant.
Mix in coconut milk
and season with fish sauce and palm sugar.
Bring to boil.
Add roasted ground peanuts,
evaporated milk and kaffir lime leaves.
Let mixture boil again
and pour sauce over seafood.
Garnish with chilli and kaffir lime leaf shreds.

### SERVES 4.

# KUNG PHAT ASPARAGUS
## FRIED PRAWNS WITH ASPARAGUS

### INGREDIENTS:

1  cup asparagus (cut to 2" lengths)
8  prawns (cleaned and shelled)
1  tbsp chopped garlic
2  tbsp vegetable oil
1  tbsp oyster sauce
2  tsp Maggi sauce
2  tsp sugar
2  tsp soy sauce
1/4  tsp salt
1/2  tsp ground pepper

### PREPARATION:

In a frying pan with 2 tbsp. vegetable oil fry
chopped garlic till golden.

Add asparagus and stir-fry
over high heat for 2 mins.
Add in shelled prawns and season
with oyster sauce, Maggi sauce, sugar,
soy sauce, salt and ground pepper.

Stir fry over high heat till prawns are cooked
and remove from stove.
Serve hot.

### SERVES 4.

# MASSAYA
## FISH FILLET SALAD

### INGREDIENTS:

10 ozs white fish fillets
(sliced across grain into 2" x 5" pieces)
1/2 cup chinese celery (cut to 2" length)
1/4 cup spring onions (cut to 2" length)
1/4 cup sliced shallots
mint leaves for garnish
1 tomato sliced for garnish

### PREPARATION:

Cook fish fillets in microwave with
full power for 2 mins.
Line a serving plate with chinese celery
and spring onions.
Place fish fillets on plate and garnish
with sliced tomatoes,
sliced shallots and mint leaves.
Serve with sauce.

### SAUCE
### INGREDIENTS:

5 yellow chillies (de-seed and slice)
1 tbsp sliced garlic
5 tbsp lime juice
4 tbsp fish sauce
1 tbsp sugar

### PREPARATION:

Mix yellow chillies and garlic in a mortar and
pound till fine. Remove chilli paste and mix with
lime juice, fish sauce and
sugar in a small mixing bowl.
Stir till sugar dissolves and serve with fish fillets.

### SERVES 4.

# LUK CHIN KUNG THOD
## PRAWN BALLS

### INGREDIENTS:

2 1/2 cups shelled shrimp (chopped)
1/4 cup pork fat (minced)
3 tbsp wheat flour
1/2 tsp baking powder
2 tsp ground pepper
2 tsp salt
1 tbsp sesame oil
2 tsp sugar
1 tbsp chopped spring onions
2 cups bread crumbs
vegetable oil for deep-frying

### PREPARATION:

In a mixing bowl, mix chopped shrimp,
minced pork fat, wheat flour,
baking powder, ground pepper, salt, sesame oil,
sugar and chopped spring onions together.

Beat the mixture together to form an elastic
paste. Refrigerate for 1 hour before
forming into 1" balls.

Roll prawn balls in bread crumbs.
Half fill a wok with vegetable oil and
drop prawn balls into moderately hot oil.
Fry till golden and crisp.

Drain with perforated spoon and stick prawn
balls on a wooden skewer with pickles.

### SERVES 4.

# YAM SALAD POO
## FRUIT SALAD WITH CRAB MEAT

### INGREDIENTS:

1/4  cup whole kernel corn
1  orange (peel and cut into thin wedges)
1/2 cup  watermelon balls
5  pineapple rings in syrup (cut into pieces)
10  lychees in syrup (cut into halves)
1/2  cup steamed crab meat
1/4  cup roasted cashew nuts
2  tbsp roasted ground dried prawns
1/4  cup cooked thick coconut milk
1/4  cup roasted grated coconut
cilantro sprigs and chilli shreds for garnish

### PREPARATION:

In a salad bowl, arrange corn, orange wedges,
watermelon balls, pineapple, lychees,
roasted coconut, roasted ground prawns,
cashew nuts and crab meat.
Top with thick coconut milk and garnish with
cilantro sprigs and chilli shreds.

Serve with spicy chilli sauce.

### SAUCE
### INGREDIENTS:

2  tbsp fish sauce
2  tbsp lime juice
1  tbsp sugar
2  tbsp roasted chilli paste (nam phrik phao)
1  tbsp hot chillies (smashed)

### PREPARATION:

In a small mixing bowl, mix sauce ingredients
together till sugar dissolves.

Serve with crab meat salad.

### SERVES 4.

# KUNG KAP
# SAUCE SAM SEE
## THREE SAUCE PRAWNS

### INGREDIENTS:

4  big prawns
4  tbsp chopped cilantro
4  tbsp chopped garlic
1/4  cup tomato sauce
1  tsp hot chillies (chopped)
1  tbsp chilli sauce
1  tbs ground pepper
1  tbsp sugar
2  tsp rice vinegar
1/2  tsp salt
Deep-fried kale leaf shreds for garnish
vegetable oil for deep frying

### PREPARATION:

Line a serving plate with deep-fried kale shreds.

Clean prawns and cut back to de-vein
leaving shell intact.
Secure a wooden skewer into prawns to keep
them straight while frying.

Half fill a wok with oil and deep fry prawns
till cooked, about 3 mins.
Remove from oil and cool before removing
skewers from prawns.
Arrange prawns on prepared plate.

In a frying pan, add 2 tbsp oil and
fry chopped garlic till golden.
Add cilantro, hot chillies and fry till well mixed.
Add tomato sauce, chilli sauce,
ground pepper, sugar, vinegar and salt.
Cook till mixture boils.
Pour sauce over prawns.

### SERVES 4.

# PLA MEUK PHAT PHONG KARI
## FRIED SQUID WITH CURRY POWDER

### INGREDIENTS:

8 ozs squid (clean, score and
slice to 2" x 3" pieces)
1 egg (beaten)
1 tbsp corn flour
1 tbsp water
1/2 cup evaporated milk
1 tbsp soy sauce
1/2 tsp salt
2 tsp sugar
1 tsp ground pepper
1 tsp sesame oil
1 tbsp chopped garlic
2 tsp curry powder
2 tbsp roasted chilli paste (nam phrik phao)
1 tomato (cut into wedges)
2 tbsp vegetable oil
1/4 cup diced red and green bell peppers
1/4 cup sliced onions

### PREPARATION:

In a small mixing bowl, mix corn flour
and water into a paste.
Mix in beaten egg, milk, soy sauce, salt,
sugar, ground pepper
sesame oil and roasted chilli paste.

In a frying pan, with 2 tbsp vegetable oil,
fry garlic till golden.
Toss in sliced squid and fry
over high heat till squid is cooked,
do not overcook.
Mix in curry powder.
Stir in corn flour mixture.
Fry mixture over high heat till
thick, about 30 secs.
Add tomato wedges, onions and bell peppers.
Toss well and remove from stove.
Garnish with spring onion shreds and serve.

### SERVES 4.

# PLA SAI LOONG
## RAINBOW FISH

### INGREDIENTS:

1/4 cup tempura flour
1/4 cup water
10 ozs sliced white fish fillets (1" x 3" pieces)
1/2 cup asparagus (cut to 2" length)
1/4 cup diced carrots
2 tbsp green peas
2 tbsp sliced bell pepper
2 tbsp diced tomatoes
1/4 cup whole fresh mushrooms
1/4 cup baby corn (sliced diagonally)
1 tbsp chopped garlic
2 tbsp vegetable oil
1 tbsp oyster sauce
1/2 tsp Maggi sauce
1 tbsp soy sauce
2 tsp sugar
1/2 tsp ground pepper

### PREPARATION:

In a small mixing bowl, mix tempura flour and
water to a smooth paste.

Fill wok with vegetable oil till 1/2 full.
Dip sliced fish fillets into tempura batter
and deep-fry in moderately
hot oil till golden and crisp.
Drain with a perforated spoon and
set aside for later use.

Remove vegetable oil in wok, retaining only 2
tbsp. Add chopped garlic and fry till golden.
Add asparagus and sliced carrots
and stir-fry over high heat for 2 mins.

Mix in green peas, bell peppers, diced tomatoes,
mushrooms and baby corn.
Season with oyster sauce, Maggi sauce,
soy sauce, sugar and ground pepper.

Toss in crisp batter fish fillets and stir fry till
well mixed.
Remove from stove and serve.

### SERVES 4.

# KLUAI TIAO
# PHLA THALAY
## SEAFOOD AND NOODLE SALAD

### INGREDIENTS:
1 cup cooked japanese rice noodles
2 big prawns (clean and retain shell)
5 ozs squid (clean, score and cut into pieces, retain tentacles)
6 ozs sea bass (sliced into 3 1" fillets)
1/2 tsp salt
1 tsp ground pepper
1 tbsp Maggi sauce
1 tbsp finely sliced lemon grass
2 tbsp sliced shallots
2 kaffir lime leaves (shred)
4 tbsp 2" carrot strips
5 hot chillies deep-fried
mint leaves for garnish

### PREPARATION:
Mix prawns, squid and sea bass with salt, ground pepper and Maggi sauce in a mixing bowl and let marinate for 1/2 hour in refrigerator.

Grill seafood brushing with margarine till cooked.
Arrange rice noodles on a serving plate with grilled seafood.

Top noodles and seafood with sliced lemon grass, shallots, lime leaf shreds and carrot strips.
Garnish with fried chillies and mint leaves.

Serve with sauce

### SAUCE
### INGREDIENTS:
3 tbsp roasted chilli paste (nam phrik phao)
1 tbsp hot chillies (smashed)
3 tbsp lemon juice
2 tbsp fish sauce
2 tbsp sugar

### PREPARATION:
In a small mixing bowl, mix the above ingredients together until sugar dissolves.
Serve with noodles and seafood.

### SERVES 4.

# MEANG KUNG SOT
# KAP PHAK KAD
## SPICY PRAWN SALAD WITH RADISH

### INGREDIENTS:
1 cup cooked prawns
1/4 cup 1" ginger shreds
1/4 cup roasted peanuts
1/4 cup 1" carrot strips
3 tbsp whole hot chillies
2 tbsp fried shallots
2 tbsp fried garlic
6 ozs white radish, sliced into 3" diameter pieces

### PREPARATION:
Arrange lettuce on a serving plate.
Soak sliced radish till crisp and drain.

On top of each round piece of radish arrange cooked prawns, ginger shreds, roasted peanuts, carrot strips, a piece of chilli, fried shallots and garlic.
Top with a marble size dab of meang (see below).

Place radish maengs on lettuce lined serving plate.

### MEANG
### INGREDIENTS:
1/4 cup dried prawns (ground)
2 tbsp sliced shallots
2 tbsp sliced garlic
1 1/2 cups roasted grated white coconut
1 cup palm sugar
1 cup tamarind juice
1/2 cup fish sauce
4 tbsp vegetable oil

### PREPARATION:
In a frying pan, fry shallots and garlic with vegetable oil till fragrant.

Season with palm sugar, fish sauce and tamarind juice.
Add roasted white coconut and ground dried prawns.
Cook till mixture thickens.
Cool and roll into marble sized balls.

### SERVES 6.

# NAM CHIM THALAY
## SEAFOOD SAUCES

## SEAFOOD SAUCE (1)

### INGREDIENTS:

2 tbsp hot chillies, finely cut
2 tbsp garlic, chopped
2 tbsp coriander root, minced
1/4 cup lime juice
1 tsp salt
1 tbsp sugar

### PREPARATION:

1. Mix the above ingredients together and use sauce for seafood recipes that require grilling, boiling, steaming or baking.

2. This sauce is also suitable for chicken and pork recipes.

## SEAFOOD SAUCE(2)

### INGREDIENTS:

2 tbsp yellow chillies, chopped
1 tbsp garlic, chopped
1 tbsp coriander root, chopped
1 tsp salt
1 tbsp sugar
1/4 cup vinegar

### PREPARATION:

1. Mix the above ingredients in a food processer and blend till smooth.

2. This sauce is good for seafood recipes that require baking, deep-frying or grilling. It is a good sauce to be eaten with Teochew porridge.

## SEAFOOD SAUCE(3)

### INGREDIENTS:

1 cup sugar
1 cup plum juice
4 plums, remove pits
1/2 cup vinegar
1 tsp salt

### PREPARATION:

1. Mash plums.

2. In a small pot, mix sugar, plum juice, vinegar and salt together.

3. Bring mixture to boil till syrup thickens and condenses.

4. Add in mashed plum and cool before bottling. Can be kept refrigerated for a period of 3 months.

5. This sauce is good with seafood recipes that require deep-frying.

6. Tomato sauce can be added if desired.

# SEAFOOD SAUCE(4)

**INGREDIENTS:**

1 cup sugar
1 cup vinegar
1 tsp salt
2 tbsp garlic, chopped
5 tbsp chillies, chopped

**PREPARATION:**

1. In a mortar, grind garlic
and chillies to a fine paste.

2. In a small pot, mix sugar, vinegar and salt
together and bring to boil till syrup thickens
and condenses.

3. Add in chilli mixture and mix well.

4. This sauce is good for seafood recipes that
requires deep-frying, steaming or baking.

5. Ground roasted peanuts and sliced cucumber
can be added and served with
fish cakes or baked rice.

# SEAFOOD SAUCE(5)

**INGREDIENTS:**

1 cup tamarind juice
4 tbsp palm sugar
2 tbsp fish sauce
20 deep-fried hot chillies
2 tbsp fried shallots
cilantro sprigs for garnishing

**PREPARATION:**

1. In a pot, mix tamarind juice, palm sugar
and fish sauce together.

2. Bring to boil till mixture thickens
and condenses.

3. Add in fried chillies and fried shallots.

4. Cool and garnish with cilantro sprigs.

5. This sauce is good with seafood recipes that
require grilling, baking or deep-frying.

6. Roasted sesame seeds can be added if desired.

# LON POO THALAY KAP PHAK SOT
## CRAB SAUCE WITH FRESH VEGETABLES

### INGREDIENTS:

2 crabs (clean, steam and remove meat)
1/4 cup sliced shallots
1 cup thick coconut milk
1/4 cup red, green and yellow chillies
(cut into pieces)
1 tbsp palm sugar
2 tbsp fish sauce
2 tbsp tamarind juice

### PREPARATION:

In a small pot, boil coconut milk with shallots.
Season with palm sugar, fish sauce
and tamarind juice.
Mix in crab meat, chilli pieces
stirring to prevent burning.
Simmer till mixture thickens and
remove from stove.
Serve with an assortment of fresh vegetables.

**SERVES 4.**

# KUNG SAWAN
## HEAVENLY PRAWNS

### INGREDIENTS:

5 big prawns
2 tbsp soaked dried chillies (cut into pieces)
4 tbsp fried garlic
4 tbsp fried shallots
1 tbsp finely sliced lemon grass
1 tbsp roasted shrimp paste
1 tbsp palm sugar
3 tbsp fish sauce
1 tbsp tamarind juice
2 tbsp lime juice
mint leaves, hot chillies, roasted cashew nuts,
raw papaya shreds, shredded kaffir lime leaves,
chilli strips and cilantro sprigs for garnish.

### PREPARATION:

In a mortar, grind fried garlic, shallots, lemon
grass and dried chillies to a fine paste
and add in shrimp paste.
Mix in palm sugar, fish sauce, tamarind juice
and lime juice.

Grill prawns brushing with
margarine till cooked.

Remove shells.
Cutting each prawn from the back
slice open to form a pocket.
Fill pocket with spicy mixture and
arrange on a serving plate.

Garnish with hot chillies, roasted cashew nuts,
raw papaya shreds, kaffir lime leaves,
chilli strips and cilantro sprigs.
Serve.

**SERVES 4.**

# KANOM JEEN NAM YA
## RICE NOODLES WITH SEAFOOD SAUCE

### SHRIMP CHILLI PASTE INGREDIENTS:

1 1/2 cups shelled shrimp
(de-veined and minced)
1 oz grilled salted fish
7 soaked dried chillies
1 tsp salt
1 tsp sliced galangal
1 tbsp lemon grass (sliced)
3 tbsp chopped shallots
1/4 cup chopped garlic
1/4 cup sliced karchai

### PREPARATION:

In a mortar, grind the above ingredients (except
minced shrimp) to a fine paste.

Mix minced shrimps with chilli paste.

### OTHER INGREDIENTS:

2 cups cooked japanese noodles
10 large prawns, cooked
4 cups coconut milk
1 cup shrimp chilli paste (see above)
1 cup prawn stock
2 tbsp fish sauce
1 tbsp palm sugar
bean sprouts, carrot strips,
cucumber shreds, yard long beans,
fried chillies, fried shallots and
red and green chilli slices for garnish.

### PREPARATION:

In a medium pot mix coconut milk and prawn
stock and bring to boil. Add in prawn chilli
paste, stirring all the time to prevent burning.
Season with fish sauce and palm sugar, stirring
until mixture boils and thickens.
Arrange rice noodles on a serving plate
with the above vegetables
and top with hot nam ya sauce.

### SERVES 4.

# PASTA NAM PHRIK PHAO THALAY
## PASTA WITH SEAFOOD CHILLI SAUCE

### INGREDIENTS:

1/4 cup shelled prawns
5 oz sliced fish fillets
1/4 cup shelled scallops
4 crab claws (smashed)
2 cups cooked spaghetti
1/4 cup roasted chilli paste (nam phrik phao)
2 tbsp chopped garlic
2 tbsp hot chillies (smashed)
1/4 cup chinese celery (cut to 1" pieces)
3 tbsp vegetable oil
3 red, green and yellow chillies (sliced)
2 tomatoes (cut to wedges)
1/4 cup sliced onions
2 tbsp sugar
1 tbsp Maggi sauce
omelette shreds for garnish

### PREPARATION:

In a wok, fry chopped garlic with
vegetable oil till golden.
Season with Maggi sauce and sugar.
Add shelled prawns, fish fillets, scallops
and crab claws and fry over high heat for 1 min.

Add chinese celery, chillies,
tomato wedges, sliced onions
and cooked spaghetti.
Fry for another minute.

Remove from stove, garnish
with omelette shreds and serve.

### SERVES 4.

# KUNG KROB PHAT MEDMAMUANG
## PRAWNS FRIED WITH CASHEW NUTS

### INGREDIENTS:

10 big prawns, clean and shell retaining tail
1 cup wheat flour
1 tsp salt
1 tbsp corn flour
1 tbsp sugar
1/4 cup cold water
1/4 cup diced bell peppers
1/4 cup diced onions
1/4 cup roasted cashew nuts
1/4 cup deep-fried chillies (cut into pieces)
1/2 cup tomato sauce
1/4 cup chilli sauce
2 tbsp sugar
1 tsp salt
1 tsp ground pepper
1 tbsp rice vinegar
2 tsp sesame oil
1 tbsp whisky
sufficient vegetable oil for deep frying

### PREPARATION

In a mixing bowl combine wheat flour,
corn flour, salt, sugar and water
together until smooth.

Dip prawns into mixed batter and deep fry in a
pan of hot oil till golden. Drain.

Place 2 tbsp of vegetable oil in frying pan and
stir-fry bell peppers and onions till fragrant.
Season with tomato sauce, chilli sauce,
sugar, salt, ground pepper, rice vinegar,
sesame oil and whisky.
Stir-fry over high heat till fragrant and
add roasted cashew nuts.
Add deep fried prawns and chillies.
Toss well and remove from stove.

### SERVES 4.

# CHU CHEE SALMON
## SALMON WITH RED CURRY

### INGREDIENTS:

2 tbsp vegetable oil
4 1/2" thick salmon steaks
2 cups thick coconut milk
1/4 cup red chilli paste
2 tbsp fish sauce
1 tbsp palm sugar
1/4 cup finely diced carrots
1/4 cup green peas
shredded kaffair lime leaves
and chilli shreds for garnish

### PREPARATION:

In a frying pan with the vegetable oil
fry chilli paste till fragrant.
Mix in thick coconut milk and add
salmon steaks, carrots and peas.
Simmer over low heat till thick.
Season with fish sauce and palm sugar
and remove from stove.
Garnish with lime leaves and chilli shreds.

### SERVES 4.

# PHAT PRA KAPHONG PREAW WAN
## SWEET AND SOUR SEA BASS

### INGREDIENTS:
9 ozs sea bass (cut into 3 thick fillets)
1/2 cup wheat flour
1 tbsp vegetable oil
1/2 tsp salt
2 tsp sugar
1 cup cold water
vegetable oil for deep frying

### PREPARATION:
Rub fish fillets with a dash of salt and pepper.
In a bowl, mix wheat flour, vegetable oil, salt,
sugar and water to a smooth batter.
Dip fish fillets into batter and deep fry fish fillets
in a pan of hot oil till crisp and golden.
Arrange on a serving plate.

### SAUCE
4 tbsp preserved ginger (shredded)
1 tbsp chopped garlic
2 tbsp red chilli (ground)
2 tbsp tomato sauce
2 tbsp rice vinegar
2 tbsp Worcestershire sauce
1 tsp fish sauce
2 tbsp sugar
2 tsp vegetable oil
3/4 cup chicken stock
1 tsp ground pepper
1 tbsp corn flour
2 tbsp water
chopped spring onions
and chilli shreds for garnish

### PREPARATION:
Put vegetable oil in frying pan and
fry garlic till fragrant.
Stir in ginger, red chilli and tomato sauce.
Season with rice vinegar, Worcestershire sauce,
fish sauce, sugar, chicken stock
and ground pepper. Bring to a boil.
Mix corn flour with water and
add to boiling sauce.
Simmer till thick. Remove from stove
and pour over crisp fish. Garnish
with spring onions and chilli shreds.

**SERVES 4.**

# PHAT PHAK RUAM MIT KAP HOI SHELL
## FRIED VEGETABLES WITH SCALLOPS

### INGREDIENTS:
1/4 cup baby corn (sliced diagonally)
1/4 cup broccoli (cut to florets)
1 tomato (cut into wedges)
1/4 cup abalone mushrooms (cut into pieces)
1/4 cup asparagus (cut to 2" pieces)
1/4 cup diced carrots
1/4 cup shelled scallops
1 tbsp chopped garlic
3 tbsp vegetable oil
2 tsp sugar
1 tbsp Maggi sauce
1 tbsp oyster sauce
1 tsp ground pepper
1/4 cup chicken stock

### PREPARATION:

In a frying pan add vegetable oil
and fry garlic till fragrant.
Add baby corn, broccoli, tomato wedges,
abalone mushrooms, asparagus and diced carrots.
Stir-fry over high heat for 2 mins or until cooked.

Add scallops and stir-fry over high heat
for another 30 seconds.
Add chicken stock
and season with soy sauce, sugar,
Maggi sauce and ground pepper.
Remove from stove and serve.

**SERVES 4.**

THE VEGETARIAN TASTE
OF THAILAND

# KAENG KUA PHAK RUAM KAP KAN CHIANG POO
## VEGETABLE AND CRAB CLAW CURRY

### INGREDIENTS:

1/2  cup pumpkin of 1" squares
1/2  cup wax gourd of 1" squares
1/2  cup yard long beans of 2" pieces
1/2  cup baby corn of 2" pieces
1/2  cup asparagus of 2" pieces
1/2  cup carrot strips of 2" pieces
2  cups crab claws (smashed)
1/4  cup chilli paste (see below)
2  cups coconut milk
2  cups thick coconut milk
2  tbsp fish sauce
1  tbsp palm sugar
2  tbsp vegetable oil

### PREPARATION:

In a medium pot add vegetable oil
and fry chilli paste till fragrant.
Add in coconut milk and simmer till boiling.
Add pumkin, wax gourd, yard long beans,
baby corn, asparagus, carrot strips
and crab claws. When mixture boils,
add thick coconut milk.
Season with fish sauce and palm sugar.

### CURRY SAUCE INGREDIENTS:

5 dry chillies (soaked)
1  tsp salt
1  tsp sliced galangal
1  tbsp sliced lemon grass
1/2  tsp rind of kaffir lime
1/2  tsp whole pepper corns
1  tbsp chopped coriander root
2  tbsp chopped shallots
3  tbsp chopped garlic
1  tsp shrimp paste
2  tbsp ground dry shrimps

### PREPARATION:

In a mortar, pound the above ingredients
together to a fine paste. Use as required.
Mix with vegetables and crab claws and serve.

### SERVES 6.

# PLA MUEK KHAI NENG MA-NAO
## STEAMED CUTTLEFISH IN LIME SAUCE

### INGREDIENTS:

2  6 oz cuttlefish fillets (clean, score on top
and retain shape and membrane)
2  slices lemon grass
6  slices galangal
2  kaffir lime leaves (torn)
2  tbsp sliced shallots
1  tbsp hot chillies (deep-fried)
2  cups chicken stock
2  tbsp chopped cilantro for garnish
lime chilli sauce

### PREPARATION:

In a medium pot, add sliced lemon grass,
galangal, kaffir lime leaves, shallots
and chicken stock. Bring to boil.
Add in cuttlefish and cook for 10 mins.
Remove cuttlefish and place on a
serving plate to be
topped with lime chilli sauce. *
Garnish with cilantro and fried chillies.

### SERVES 4.

*see seafood sauce (1) on page 116

# MASSAMAN KUNG YAI
## CURRY PRAWNS

### INGREDIENTS:

6  big prawns
4  cups coconut milk
1/4  cup roasted ground peanuts
5  shallots
3  cardamon seed pods
3  bay leaves (torn)
1/4  cup curry paste (see below)
2  tbsp fish sauce
1  tbsp palm sugar
2  tbsp tamarind juice
5  hard boiled eggs
2  tbsp vegetable oil

### PREPARATION:

In a wok, add vegetable oil. Fry curry
paste over low fire till fragrant.
Mix in coconut milk and simmer till boiling.
Add in prawns, roasted ground peanuts,
shallots, cardamon and bay leaves.
Season with fish sauce, palm sugar, and
tamarind juice and bring to boil again.
Add eggs and remove from stove.
Serve hot.

### CURRY PASTE INGREDIENTS:

1  tbsp coriander seeds
1  tsp cumin seeds
2  cloves
6  dried chillies (soaked)
1  tsp salt
1  tsp galangal (chopped)
1  tbsp sliced lemon grass
4  tbsp shallots
3  tbsp sliced garlic
1  tsp shrimp paste (roasted)

### PREPARATION:

In a small frying pan, dry roast coriander seeds,
cumin seeds, and cloves together till fragrant.
In a mortar, mix roasted spices, dry chillies, salt,
galangal, sliced lemon grass, shallots, garlic
and shrimp paste together and pound till fine.
Use as required.
**SERVES 4.**

# KUNG THOD SOT SAI POO
## CRAB STUFFED PRAWNS

### INGREDIENTS:

20  prawns (clean, shell and de-vein,
retain tail)
1  cup steamed crab meat
1/2  cup minced pork
1/4  cup ham (shredded)
1  tbsp chopped spring onions
2  tbsp sliced onions
1  tsp ground pepper
2  tsp sesame oil
1  tsp salt
1  tbsp sugar
1  tbsp Maggi sauce
1  cup wheat flour
2  eggs
2  cups bread crumbs
sufficient vegetable oil for deep-frying

### PREPARATION:

Mix crab, minced pork, shredded ham,
chopped spring onions, shallots, ground pepper,
sesame oil, salt, sugar and Maggi sauce
in a small mixing bowl till well blended.
Slice along the back of each prawn
to form a pocket.
Stuff filling into backs of prepared prawns.
Break eggs into a mixing bowl, dip stuffed
prawns and coat with breadcrumbs.
Half fill a wok with vegetable oil and deep fry
stuffed prawns till golden.
Drain and serve.

### SERVES 4.

# KWAY JAP THALAY SHANGHAI
### SHANGHAI NOODLES IN SEAFOOD BROTH

### INGREDIENTS:
5 shelled prawns
4 oz squid (clean, score and cut into pieces)
5 shelled mussels
2 crab claws (smashed)
4 oz sliced white fish fillet
1 cup shanghai sheet noodles
1 cup chinese cabbage (cut into pieces)
1 cup lettuce (cut into pieces)
1 tbsp salted radish (tang chye)
1 tbsp sugar
2 tbsp Maggi sauce
1 tbsp soy sauce
1/2 tsp salt
1 tsp pepper
4 cups chicken stock
chopped spring onions, 1" length chinese celery
and fried garlic for garnish

### PREPARATION:
In a medium pot, add chicken stock, salted
radish, sugar, Maggi sauce, soy sauce,
salt and pepper. Bring to boil.
Add prawns, squid, mussels,
crab claws and fish fillets.
Add in shanghai sheet noodles, chinese cabbage
to cook for about 1 min.
Line a soup bowl with lettuce.
Carefully spoon hot soup over lettuce.

### TAO CHEO SAUCE
### INGREDIENTS:
3 tbsp ground salted fermented beans
1 tbsp garlic (chopped)
1 tbsp hot chillies (chopped)
2 tsp sugar
1 tsp vinegar

### PREPARATION:
Mix the above ingredients together to be served
with shanghai sheet noodles in broth.

### SERVES 2.

# YAM THALAY
### SPICY SEAFOOD SALAD

### INGREDIENTS:

5 shelled prawns (retain tail)
4 red snapper fillets (2" x 3" slices)
4 scallops
1/2 cup 3" cucumber strips
1/2 cup 2" carrot strips
1/2 cup 2" mango strips
2 tbsp siced shallots
roasted cashew nuts, mint leaves and
sliced shallots for garnish

### PREPARATION

Place prawns, fish fillets and scallops
in a pot of boiling water till cooked,
about 1 min. Drain.
In a bowl, mix carrot, mango and
cucumber strips together.
Toss in cooked seafood and add sauce.
Toss mixture well and
garnish with cashew nuts, mint leaves
and sliced shallots.

### SAUCE

3 tbsp lime juice
2 tbsp fish sauce
1 tbsp palm sugar
2 tbsp hot chillies (smashed)

### PREPARATION:

In a small mixing bowl, mix sauce ingredients
together till well blended.

### SERVES 4.

# NAM PHRIK TUA DAENG
## RED BEAN CHILLI PASTE WITH RICE

### CHILLI PASTE
**INGREDIENTS:**
1/4 cup ground dried prawns
3 tbsp fish sauce
1/4 cup palm sugar
1/4 cup tamarind juice
1/2 cup vegetable oil
1/2 cup cooked red beans
1/2 cup fried shallots
1/2 cup fried garlic
1/4 cup fried chillies
1/4 cup fried hot chillies
1 tsp shrimp paste

### PREPARATION:
In a mortar, pound red beans, shallots, garlic,
chillies and shrimp paste to a fine paste.
In a frying pan, fry ground paste
with vegetable oil till fragrant
and add in dried prawns.
Season with fish sauce, sugar
and tamarind juice. Stir fry mixture
till well mixed and remove from stove.

### RICE
**INGREDIENTS:**
2 cups cooked rice
1/2 cup yard long beans (shredded)
1 tbsp hot chillies (finely sliced)
1/4 cup omelette shreds

### PREPARATION:
Mix the above in a mixing bowl and press rice
mixture into a small bowl to from a mound.
Remove rice mounds from bowl and arrange
on a serving plate.

### OTHER INGREDIENTS:
2 eggs
5 1" x 3" red snapper fillets
10 2" yard long beans
10 2" baby corn
10 2" asparagus
vegetable oil for deep frying

### PREPARATION:
Break eggs into a small mixing bowl.
Heat oil in a wok.
Dip vegetables and fish fillets into beaten egg
and deep fry until golden. Serve with
rice and red bean chilli paste.

**SERVES 4.**

# PLA MEUK THOD
## CRISPY CUTTLEFISH

**INGREDIENTS:**
2 lbs cuttlefish (clean and cut into
1" x 3" thick pieces)
2 eggs (beaten)
1/2 cup wheat flour
2 cups bread crumbs
2 tsp ground pepper
2 tsp sugar
1 tsp salt
2 tsp sesame oil
1 tbsp Maggi sauce

### PREPARATION:
In a mixing bowl, combine
cuttlefish with ground pepper, sugar,
salt, sesame oil and Maggi sauce.
Marinate for 1/2 hour.
Coat marinated cuttlefish pieces with
wheat flour, dip into beaten eggs
and coat with bread crumbs.
Fill a wok with oil for deep-frying,
heat till warm and deep
fry cuttlefish till golden and crisp.
Drain and arrange on a serving plate.
Serve with sauce.

### SAUCE
**INGREDIENTS:**
2 tbsp red chillies (ground)
1 tbsp chopped garlic
1 cup rice vinegar
1 cup sugar
1 tsp salt

### PREPARATION:
In a small pot boil vinegar,
sugar and salt together.
Add ground chillies and chopped garlic.
Simmer till thick. Remove from stove.
Serve with fried cuttlefish.

**SERVES 4.**

# YAM JAO THALAY
## SPICY SHELLFISH SALAD

### INGREDIENTS:

1/2 cup shelled scallops
1/2 cup shelled oysters
1/2 cup shelled mussels
1/4 cup shredded hard boiled egg whites
2 tbsp sliced garlic
2 tbsp sliced shallots
1/2 cup coconut cream
1/4 cup roasted ground peanuts
mint leaves, cilantro sprigs
and chilli strips for garnish
sea shells to hold seafood mixture

### PREPARATION:

Bring a small pot of water to boil.
Cook scallops, oysters and mussels
for 1 min and drain.
In a bowl mix cooked seafood,
shredded egg whites, garlic, shallots and
ground peanuts together with sauce (see below).
Toss well.
Fill mixture into scallop shells and
top with coconut cream.
Garnish with mint leaves
and cilantro sprigs.

### SAUCE
### INGREDIENTS:

1/4 cup roasted chilli paste
(nam phrik phao)
1/4 cup lime juice
1 tbsp sugar
3 tbsp fish sauce
2 tbsp chopped hot chillies

### PREPARATION:

Mix the above ingredients together
in a mixing bowl. Use as required

### SERVES 4.

# KALAM PEE SAWEY
## SPICY CABBAGE SALAD

### INGREDIENTS:

1 cup cabbage (shredded)
1/2 cup cooked crab meat
1/4 cup shelled cooked prawns
1 tomato (cut to wedges)
1/4 cup roasted peanuts
1/4 cup yard long beans (cut into 2" pieces)
1 tbsp hot chillies
2 tbsp garlic
1 tbsp dried shrimp
2 tbsp fish sauce
1 tbsp palm sugar
3 tbsp lime juice
lettuce for garnish

### PREPARATION:

In a mortar, coarsely grind
chillies and garlic.
In a bowl mix yard long beans, dried shrimp
and roasted peanuts. Season with fish sauce,
palm sugar and lime juice.
Mix well.
Line a serving plate with lettuce and top with
shredded cabbage, cooked crab meat, cooked
prawns and tomato wedges.
Top with pounded chilli and garlic mixture
and serve.

### SERVES 4.

# RUAM MIT CHAN LAWN
## MIXED SEAFOOD HOT PLATE

### INGREDIENTS:

1/4  cup squid (clean, remove membrane,
score and slice into pieces)
1/4  cup shelled prawns (clean and retain tail)
1/4  cup red snapper (cut into 2" cubes)
1/4  cup chicken liver (cut into pieces)
1/4  cup chicken breast (sliced)
2  tbsp oyster sauce
2  tsp soy sauce
1  tbsp Maggi sauce
1  tsp ground pepper
2  tsp sugar
2  tbsp Chinese wine
1  tbsp sesame oil
1/2  cup chicken stock
1  tbsp corn flour
1  tbsp water
4  tbsp vegetable oil
2  tbsp chopped garlic

### PREPARATION

In a small bowl, mix corn flour
and water together.
Boil a small pot of water and immerse
squid, prawns, fish, chicken livers
and sliced chicken breast.
Cook for 1 min in boiling water and drain.
Pour vegetable oil into a wok and
fry garlic till fragrant.
Add cooked meat to wok and season with soy
sauce, Maggi sauce, pepper, sugar, sesame oil,
Chinese wine and chicken stock.
Let simmer, add corn flour mixture
and stir-fry until  mixture binds together.
Serve immediately on a prepared hot platter.

### SERVES 4.

# KANG CHIANG POO SONG KRUENG
## STUFFED CRAB CLAWS

### INGREDIENTS:

1/2  cup minced pork
1/2  cup chopped prawns
1  cup steamed crab meat
1  tbsp coriander root
1  tbsp chopped garlic
2  tsp pepper corns
2  tbsp spring onions
2  tsp sugar
1/2  tsp salt
2  tsp Maggi sauce
2  tsp soy sauce
1  tbsp oyster sauce
2  tsp sesame oil
2  eggs (beaten)
2  cups breadcumbs
12  crab claws
vegetable oil for deep-frying

### PREPARATION:

In a mortar, pound coriander root,
garlic and pepper till fine.
Remove from mortar and place in a mixing bowl.
Add chopped prawns, crab
and minced pork.
Mix in pepper, sugar, salt, Maggi sauce,
oyster sauce and sesame oil.
Beat mixture until smooth.
Refrigerate for 1 hour before using.

Remove mixture from refrigerator
and wrap each crab claw with
about 1 oz of mixture.
Dip wrapped crab claws in beaten eggs and
coat with breadcrumbs.
Deep fry in moderately hot oil
till golden brown and crisp.
Serve with fish sauce (see pages 116 and 117)
and pickled vegetables.

### SERVES 6.

# SALAT SEAFOOD
## SEAFOOD SALAD

### INGREDIENTS:
1/4 cup squid (clean, remove membrane and
cut into rings)
1/4 cup prawns, shell and retain tail
1 hard boiled egg (sliced)
1/4 cup diced cooked potatoes
1 cup salad greens
1/4 cup coarsely diced onions
1/4 cup cucumber (remove core and thinly
slice lengthwise)
10 pieces lettuce
salad greens for garnish

### PREPARATION:
Bring a small pot of water to boil.
Cook squid and prawns for 1 min. Drain.
Line a platter with lettuce and salad greens.
Top with cooked seafood,
sliced egg, potatoes, tomatoes,
cucumber and onions.
Serve with sauce.

### SAUCE
2 tsp hot chillies
2 cloves garlic
3 tbsp lime juice
3 tbsp palm sugar
2 tbsp fish sauce
4 tbsp peanut butter

### SAUCE
### PREPARATION:
Pound hot chillies and garlic
in a mortar till fine.
In a bowl combine ground mixture,
peanut butter, lime juice,
palm sugar and fish sauce.
Mix to a smooth paste.
Serve with seafood salad.

### SERVES 4.

# PIAE-SA KUNG
## SPICY SEAFOOD SOUP

### INGREDIENTS:
3 big prawns (cleaned)
1 cup Chinese cabbage (cut into pieces)
1/4 cup spring onions (cut to 1" length)
1/4 cup Chinese celery (cut 1" length)
1 cup soft bean curd (cut into big pieces)
2 preserved plums
1 tbsp preserved plum juice
2 tbsp lime juice
4 cups chicken stock
2 tsp hot chillies (smashed)
10 pieces garlic (smashed)
1 tsp ground pepper
2 tbsp sugar
2 tbsp fish sauce
4 tbsp young ginger (shredded) and
sliced chillies for garnish

### PREPARATION:
Arrange Chinese cabbage, spring onions and
Chinese celery in a serving bowl.
In a medium pot bring chicken stock,
hot chillies and smashed garlic to boil.
Add ground pepper, sugar,
fish sauce, preserved plums,
preserved plum juice and prawns.
Simmer till prawns are cooked, about 15 mins.
Remove prawns from soup and arrange
in the serving bowl with bean curd.
Add lime juice to soup and remove from heat.
Pour hot soup into serving bowl.
Garnish with sliced ginger and chillies.
Serve hot.

### SERVES 4.

# SOUP LAWN POO
## CRAB SOUP

### INGREDIENTS:
1 cup crab meat
1/4 cup diced asparagus
1/4 cup mushrooms
2 tbsp green peas
1/4 cup hard bean curd (cut into cubes)
1/4 cup diced tomatos
4 cups chicken stock
2 tsp Worcestershire sauce
2 tsp Maggi sauce
1/2 tsp salt
1 tbsp soy sauce
2 tsp sugar
1 tsp ground pepper
2 tbsp corn flour
2 tbsp water

### PREPARATION:
Mix corn flour with water. Pour chicken stock
into a medium sized pot and bring to boil.
Add diced asparagus, mushrooms, green peas,
bean curd and tomatoes. Simmer for 5 mins and
add Worcestershire sauce, salt,
soy sauce, Maggi sauce, sugar, ground pepper
and corn flour mixture.
Boil until soup thickens
Add crab meat.
Serve hot.

### SERVES 4.

# PRA NNG PRA THONG
## GOLD FISH CAKES

### INGREDIENTS:
1/2 cup chopped shrimp
1 cup fresh diced mackerel
1/4 cup minced pork fat
1 tsp salt
2 tsp sugar
1 tbsp Maggi sauce
10 cleaned duck feet webs
sufficient green peas for eyes
and carrot pieces for fins

### PREPARATION:
Place fish, chopped prawns and minced pork fat on a
chopping board. With a cleaver mince
the mixture together until fine.
Place mixture in a bowl with salt,
sugar and Maggi sauce.
Blend mixture with hand until it binds together.
Mould each fish body using a lightly oiled chinese
porcelain tablespoon. Remove and assemble "fish"
with duck's web to resemble fish tail, green peas to
resemble eyes and carrots to resemble fins.
Place gold fish on an oiled steaming tray.
Steam over high heat for 10 mins.
Arrange gold fish on a serving plate.
Serve with sauce.

### SAUCE INGREDIENTS:
2 cups chicken stock
1/2 cup small dried Chinese mushrooms
(soaked and left whole)
2 tbsp oyster sauce
1 tbsp Maggi sauce
2 tbs soy sauce
2 tsp sugar
1 tbsp garlic (chopped)
2 tbsp vegetable oil
1 tbsp corn flour
1 tbsp water
1 tsp ground pepper

### SAUCE PREPARATION:
In a frying pan add vegetable oil
and fry garlic till fragrant.
Add stock and Chinese mushrooms. Season with
oyster sauce, Maggi sauce, soy sauce, sugar
and corn flour mixture.
Let mixture simmer till thick.
Pour sauce over gold fish and serve.

### SERVES 4.

# KAENG PHRA MEUK SOT SAI PHONLAMAI LUAM
## SQUID CURRY WITH MIXED FRUIT

### INGREDIENTS:
10 ozs small squid
1 cup cleaned prawns
1/2 cup minced pork
1 can lychees in syrup
1/4 cup green seedless grapes
1/4 cup pineapple chucks in syrup
2 tomatoes (cut into wedges)
1/4 cup red curry paste
4 cups coconut milk
2 tbsp vegetable oil
2 tbsp fish sauce
2 tbsp plam sugar
dash of salt and ground pepper
shredded kaffir lime leaves for garnish

### PREPARATION:
Clean squid and tentacles and leave whole.
Chop prawns and mix together with
minced pork adding a dash of salt and pepper.
Stuff filling into squid's body and tentacles.
In a frying pan with 2 tbsp vegetable oil
fry red curry paste till fragrant.
Add coconut milk and stuffed squid.
Simmer for 10 mins.
Add lychees, grapes, pineapple chucks
and tomatoes stiring gently.
Season with fish sauce and palm sugar.
Serve hot garnished with sliced chillies
and kaffir lime leaf shreds.

### SERVES 4.

# TOM YAM MA-KHAM PIEK
## TAMARIND TOM YAM SOUP

### INGREDIENTS:
1/2 cup small clams with shells
(soaked to remove sand)
1/4 cup squid (clean, remove membrane
and cut into rings)
5 big prawns (shelled and deveined,
retaining tail)
1/4 cup thick tamarind juice
2 tbsp fish sauce
1 tbsp palm sugar
4 cups chicken stock
1 tsp salt
2 coriander roots
5 shallots (smashed)
10 thin slices galangal
2 4" pieces lemon grass (smashed)
2 tsp ground chilli

### PREPARATION:
In a medium pot, bring chicken stock and
tamarind juice to boil and mix in ground chilli.
Add shallots, galangal,
lemon grass and coriander roots.
Simmer for 15 mins.
Add clams, squid and big prawns.
Season with palm sugar, fish sauce and salt.
Return to simmer and remove from heat.
Serve hot.

### SERVES 4.

# SHANGHAI PHAT KEEMAO
## FRIED SPICY SHANGHAI NOODLES

### INGREDIENTS:
2 cups shanghai sheet noodles
1/4 shelled fresh prawns
1/4 cup mushrooms (cut into halves)
1/4 cup small clams in shells
1/4 cup green peas
1/4 cup baby corn (cut into half)
1/4 cup carrot strips
1/4 cup sliced cabbage
2 red chillies (sliced)
2 tbsp roasted chilli paste
(Nam Phrik phao)
2 tbsp oyster sauce
1 tbsp Maggi suace
2 tbsp sugar
1 tbsp soy sauce
2 tbsp chopped garlic
4 tbsp vegetable oil
deep fried basil leaves for topping

### PREPARATION:
In a wok with vegetable oil fry garlic
over high heat until fragrant.
Add in roasted chilli paste, prawns, clams,
shanghai sheet noodles, sliced chillies,
green peas, corn, carrot strips,
cabbage and mushrooms.
Season with oyster sauce,
Maggi sauce, sugar and soy sauce.
Stir-fry mixture over high heat for
30 seconds until well mixed.
Serve topped with basil leaves.

**SERVES 4.**

# POH PIAH SOT
## FRESH SPRING ROLLS

### INGREDIENTS:
20 fresh * spring roll skins
1 cup cooked bean sprouts
1/2 cup cooked crab meat
20 chinese sausage (cut into 2" strips)
20 cucumber sticks (skin and core)
20 cooked prawns (sliced)
1/2 cup carrot strips
1/2 cup sliced pork
20 cooked baby corn
1/2 cup hard bean curd cut into strips
1 tbsp soy sauce
1 tbsp Maggi sauce
1 tbsp palm sugar
1/4 cup omelette shreds
1/4 cup vegetable oil for frying

### PREPARATION
Fry chinese sausage in a wok over high heat
until fragrant, remove and drain.
Retain hot oil and fry sliced pork till cooked.
Stir in bean curd strips and season with soy sauce,
Maggi sauce and palm sugar.
Fry until well mixed. Remove from wok and cool.
Place fresh spring roll skins on a floured surface. Place
small amounts of bean sprouts, pork mixture, crab,
prawns, sausage, cucumber, corn, carrot strips
and omelette shreds on each fresh spring roll skin.
From into a roll by tucking in from both sides.
Cut pieces and arrange on a serving dish.
Top with fresh vegetables and Sauce.

### SAUCE INGREDIENTS:
2 tbsp tamarind juice
1/4 cup vinegar
1/4 cup fish sauce
1/4 cup soy sauce
1 tbsp black soy sauce
2 tbsp sesame oil
1/2 cup brown sugar
1/2 cup sugar
2 tbsp all purpose flour
2 tbsp water
1/4 cup roasted ground white sesame seeds
2 tbsp fried shallots

### SAUCE PREPARATION:
Combine flour and water to form a paste.
In a small pot mix tamarind juice, vinegar, fish sauce,
soy sauce, brown sugar, black soy sauce and sesame
oil together. Boil and add flour mixture.
Once mixture thickens
mix in roasted sesame seeds and shallots.

**SERVES 6**
* buy the white, rice flour fresh spring roll skins, not
the ones that need to be deep fried. Moisten before use.

# KHAO OP KUNG SOT
**BAKED PRAWN RICE**

### INGREDIENTS:
1 cup rice
1 1/2 cups water
1/4 tsp salt
1 cup shelled prawns
2 cups evaporated milk
1/4 tsp vinegar
1 tbsp chopped ginger
1 tbsp chopped garlic
1/2 cup diced cooked potatoes
1/4 cup green peas
2 tbsp fried shallots

### SPICE MIXTURE
1/4 tsp roasted coriander seeds
1/4 tsp roasted cumin seeds
1 tsp turmeric powder
10 pepper corns
1/8 tsp ground cinnamon
3 pcs clove
2 pcs nutmeg
1 tbsp curry powder
1 tbsp ground chilli powder
1/4 tsp salt

### PREPARATION:
Grind spices together in a mortar.
Mix evaporated milk, vinegar,
chopped ginger, garlic, salt
and ground spice mixture.
Add shelled prawns.
Marinate in the refrigerator for one hour.

Wash rice.
Combine washed rice with water,
marinated prawns,
potatoes and green peas.
Cook in a rice cooker.
Serve prawn rice topped with fried shallots.

**SERVES 2.**

# KUAI TIAO LAD PHRA KHAPONG THOD
**RICE NOODLES WITH FRIED FISH FILLETS**

### INGREDIENTS:
2 cups rice noodles
1 tbsp black soy sauce
4 pcs white fish fillets
1 cup breadcrumbs
2 eggs, beaten
1/2 cup all purpose flour
1/2 cup cooked broccoli florets
1/2 cup baby corn, sliced
1/4 cup diced carrots
1 tomato, diced
4 cups chicken stock
2 tbsp Maggi sauce
2 tbsp soy sauce
2 tbsp oyster sauce
1 tsp pepper
4 tbsp corn flour
3 tbsp water
vegetable oil for frying

### PREPARATION:
Dilute corn flour with water.
Rub fish fillets with a dash of salt
and coat with all purpose flour.
Dip fish fillets into beaten eggs
and coat with breadcrumbs.
Fill a wok with sufficient vegetable oil
to deep fry fish fillets till golden.
Remove vegetable oil from wok leaving 4 tbsp
oil. Fry rice noodles over high heat till fragrant.
Arrange noodles on a serving platter
topped with fried fish.

In a wok with 2 tbsp vegetable oil
fry garlic till fragrant.
Add broccoli, corn, carrots and tomatoes.
Fry over high heat for 1 minute.
Add chicken stock.
Season with Maggi sauce,
soy sauce, oyster sauce and pepper.
When mixture boils, stir in corn flour to thicken.
Pour over noodles.
Serve hot.

**SERVES 4.**

# NAM PHRIK KUNG SOT
## SPICY PRAWN DIP

### INGREDIENTS:
1/2 cup cooked chopped prawns
2 hot chillies, smashed
2 tbsp chopped garlic
2 tbsp roasted shrimp paste
1 tbsp chopped cilantro
2 tbsp palm sugar
2 tbsp lime juice
2 tbsp fish sauce

### PREPARATION:
In a mortar pound garlic
and shrimp paste till fine.
Mix with palm sugar, chillies,
lime juice and fish sauce.
Add chopped prawns and cilantro.
Serve with cooked rice and fresh vegetables.

**SERVES 4.**

# HOI THOD SAWEY
## FRIED OYSTERS SUPREME

### INGREDIENTS:
1 cup fresh shucked oysters
1 cup tempura flour
1 to 1 1/2 cups bean sprouts
1/2 cup carrot strips of 2" lengths
1/4 cup green peas
1/4 cup whole kernel corn
2 tbsp oyster sauce
2 tbsp Maggi sauce
1 tbsp sugar
2 tbsp chopped garlic
spring onion, chinese parsley,
sliced chillies for garnish
vegetable oil for frying

### PREPARATION:
Dilute tempura flour with water.
Dip oysters in batter and deep fry in hot
vegetable oil till crisp. Remove and drain.
Fill wok with 3 tbsp vegetable oil
and fry garlic till fragrant.
Add bean sprouts, peas, carrots and corn.
Season with Maggi sauce, oyster sauce,
sugar and soy sauce.
Stir-fry for 1 min and remove from heat.
Lastly mix in crisp oysters.
Serve hot topped with spring onions, chinese
parsely and chillies.

**SERVES 2.**

# KHAO TOM HOI SHELL
## SCALLOP PORRIDGE

### INGREDIENTS:
2 cups cooked rice
20 fresh scallops
1/2 cup diced carrots
1/4 cup green peas
2 cups chicken stock
4 tbsp soy sauce
1 tsp sugar
1 tbsp Maggi sauce
1 tbsp ginger juice
1 tsp ground pepper
2 stalks coriander root
chopped cilantro leaves
sufficient fried garlic for garnish

### PREPARATION:
Marinate scallops with ginger juice.
In a medium pot bring chicken stock and
coriander roots to boil.
Add diced carrots, peas and cooked rice. Boil
until vegetables are cooked.
Stir in scallops and cook for
one additional minute.
Season with soy sauce, sugar, Maggi sauce
and ground pepper.
Serve hot, topped with fried garlic
and chopped cilantro leaves.

### SERVES 2.

# GAENG PAR TALAY RUAMMIT
## SPICY SEAFOOD CURRY

### INGREDIENTS:
1/2 cup clams in shells
1/2 cup shelled prawns
1/2 cup scored cuttlefish pieces
1/2 cup sliced white fish fillets
1/4 cup baby corn, cut into pieces
1/4 cup diced pumpkin
1/2 cup Chinese long beans cut to 2" strips
4 pcs kaffair lime leaves
1/8 cup krachai, shredded
3 red chillies, sliced lengthwise
1/4 cup red chilli paste
1 tbsp roasted ground rice
2 tbsp fish sauce
1 tbsp sugar
4 cups stock
2 tbsp vegetable oil
fried basil leaves for garnish

### PREPARATION:
In a medium pot, fry red chilli paste
in vegetable oil till fragrant.
Add stock, lime leaves, krachai, chilli pieces,
ground rice and bring to a boil.
Season with fish sauce and sugar.
Simmer curry for 15 mins.
Add baby corn, pumpkin and long beans.
Boil for 5 mins.
Lastly, add clams, prawns,
cuttlefish and fish fillets.
Bring to a boil and remove from heat.
Serve hot topped with fried basil leaves.

### SERVES 4.

# THAI FRUITS

Thailand, a country renowned for its bountiful crops of exotic and delicious tropical fruits all year round attracts tourist from neighboring South-Asia and afar with its beauty and charm.

Fruits like bananas, coconuts, pineapples, payayas, guavas and oranges are cultivated to be enjoyed all year round.

As for seasonal exotic fruits, the demand has certainly increased, thus enabling us to savour a more varied selection during the growing season.

In the beginning of the year, we Thais are blessed with big, delicious, juicy and crisp rose apples. In early March, a variety of ripe and unripe mangoes will dominate the market. The unripe variety is divided into 2 groups, the sweet, firm and crispy mangoes and the slightly sweet and sourish variety eaten with salted chilli sugar or spicy palm sugar dips. Ripe mangoes are either eaten fresh or accompanied with sweetened glutinous rice. In mid-April, durian, the king of exotic fruits will dominate the market with its spiky fruit and pungent flavour. Once opened, the fruit reveals a fleshy crop of thick yellow pulp . The Thais prefer this delicacy, firm, sweet

155

and crisp and less pungent thus we see a great trend in cultivating the Mon-thong variety. To balance the heat after eating durian Thais eat the queen of exotic fruits, the mangosteen. This fruit is the size of a chicken egg, round, hardcovered and dark brown skinned but once opened, the inside of the thick cover reveals a purple inner layer filled with a white fleshy pulp. The white pulp is sweet and cools the human system after durian is consumed.

From the middle of the year till year's end we eat fruits like custard apples, lychees, logans, rambutans and so on, the list is endless.

Each region has its special fruits. The northern region cultivates lychees, logans and mangoes as the cool weather suits these fruits.

However the central region remains the major fruit producing area in Thailand

## Thai Desserts

It is rather difficult to tell exactly the history of Thai desserts since there is no written evidence available. Many Thai culinary experts assume that it started as early as the time when rice and coconut were first cultivated.

Flour, coconut and sugar are the three major ingredients of Thai desserts, other ingredients are added afterwards. Besides the main ingredients, natural colouring extracts such as green from screwpine, yellow from turmeric, and indigo from the butterfly pea are always added.

The most remarkably step in the history

of Thai desserts was when Lady Vichayendra introduced many new dessert recipes to the Thai people.

It has been recorded in ancient journals that Lady Vichayendra, wife of Chaopraya Vichayendra who was a European civil servant in the reign of the Great King Narai, started teaching Thai people to make desserts such as thongyod, thongyip, foithong, etc. Eventually, these recipes became Thai specialties.

The cooking techniques that lady Vichayendra taught Thai people can be considered a significant development. It was during this time that eggs were introduced into Thai dessert recipes which previously consisted only of flour, coconut and sugar. Since then, eggs are considered a major ingredient in Thai desserts.

Thai desserts also play an important role in Thai lifestyle. Besides being included in everyday menus of Thai life, they reflect Thai's way of thinking; their philosophy and culture.

Thai people have different kinds of desserts for different events. Desserts for Songkran Festival are different from those for Buddhist Lent. Household ceremonies such as weddings, housewarmings or funerals, require special kinds of desserts. The names of these desserts are the indicative factor. For example, desserts that begin with the words "Thong" (gold) or "Tien" (candle) signify a prosperous and bright future.

The belief in these blessed names are still preserved and widely practiced even in these modern days.

## KHAO NIAO MOON MAMUANG
### SWEET GLUTINOUS RICE
### WITH RIPE MANGO

### INGREDIENTS:

2 cups glutinous rice
2 cups thick coconut milk
2 tsp salt
1/4 cup sugar

### PREPARATION:

Wash glutinous rice and soak overnight.
Wash soaked glutinous rice again and
place in a piece of muslin cloth.
Steam over high heat for about 1/2 hour.
In a small pot mix thick coconut milk with salt and
sugar. Simmer over low heat for
5 mins or until sugar dissolves.
Pour coconut milk and sugar syrup over hot
cooked glutinous rice and stir with a wooden spoon
until rice and sugar mixture combines.

### COCONUT TOPPPING
### INGREDIENTS

1 cup thick coconut milk
1 tsp salt
2 tbsp rice flour

Mix ingredients in coconut topping and simmer
over low heat. Stirring constantly with a wooden
spoon until mixture thickens.

Arrange sweet glutinous rice on a serving plate
with ripe magoes or stuff rice
into jackfruit pockets.
Top with coconut cream.

### SERVES 4

## KLUAI HOM TOM CHIM MA-PHRAO
### STEAMED FRAGRANT BANANAS
### WITH COCONUT SHREDS

### INGREDIENTS:

10 slightly unripe fragrant bananas
2 cups fresh coconut, shredded
1/2 cup sugar
1/4 cup roasted ground white
and black sesame seeds
1/2 tsp salt

### PREPARATION:

Mix sugar, sesame seeds and salt together.
Steam coconut shreds in a steamer over
high heat for 5 mins or in a microwave
for 1 min at full power.
Bring a pot of water to boil and immerse
unpeeled bananas. Boil for 5 minutes.
Drain and cool before peeling and slicing.
Arrange sliced bananas on a serving plate.
Top with shredded coconut and
sesame sugar mixture.

### SERVES 4.

THE VEGETARIAN TASTE
OF THAILAND

# RUAM-MIT
## COCONUT DESSERT

### TAPIOCA STRIPS
### INGREDIENTS:
2 cups tapioca flour
1 cup boiling water
1/4 tsp pink food colouring

Mix ingredients together, stirring constantly with a wooden spoon to form dough. Knead till smooth and roll into a thin sheet on a floured surface. Cut dough into 2" strips and drop into boiling water until the strips turn clear and float. Drain. Soak in cold water until cool. Drain.

### AGAR AGAR JELLY
1 tbsp agar agar jelly powder
3 cups water
1 1/2 cups sugar

Mix agar agar powder, water and sugar in a small pot and bring to boil. When mixture boils, divide into 2 portions. Add 1/8 tsp of red food colouring to one portion and 1/8 tsp of green food colouring to the other. Pour mixtures into indivudual 5"x 5" square trays to set.

### SYRUP
3 cups sugar
3 cups water
1 cup canned jackfruit, cut into fine strips

Mix sugar and water in a small pot and simmer mixture over low heat till sugar dissolves. Immediately add in jackfruit strips to soak.

### RUAM-MIT INGREDIENTS
1 cup cooked tapioca strips
1 cup diced coloured agar agar jelly
1/2 cup canned kidney beans
1/2 cup cooked colored large sago pellets
3 cups boiled coconut milk
1 cup canned palm seeds, sliced
crushed ice

For boiled coconut milk, place fresh coconut milk in a pot and simmer over low heat for about 5 minutes. Remove from stove. To cook sago pellets, bring a pot of water to boil, add sago pellets and boil till water turns starchy and thickens. Immediately drain and wash off starch. Boil again until pellets turn clear. Wash again and drain. Pour coloured syrup into cooked sago pellets and blend well. In a large mixing bowl, mix cooled tapioca strips, kidney beans, diced agar agar jelly, coloured sago, sliced palm seeds, boiled coconut milk, jackfruit syrup and crushed ice together. Mix well and serve immediately.
**SERVES 8.**

## KLUAI HOM YANG
## KAP SAUCE
### GRILLED FRAGRANT BANANAS

### INGREDIENTS:

10 slightly unripe fragrant bananas
1 cup plam sgar
1 cup thick coconut milk
1 cup evaporated milk
2 tsp salt
1/2 tsp vanilla extract
5 tbsp corn flour
3 tbsp water
4 screwpine leaves, knoted together

### PREPARATION:

In a sauce pan combine corn flour and water.
Add remaining sauce ingredients and slowly
bring to a boil, stirring until sauce thickens.
Grill bananas in peels until skin turns brown
all over. Peel and slice grilled bananas.
Place on a serving plate and top with sauce.
Bananas must be firm and slightly yellow in
colour, if not, they will be too soft and mashy
after grilling.

### SERVES 6.

## WOON LAM YAI LOI KIAO
### STUFFED LOGAN JELLY DESSERT

### INGREDIENTS:

1 cup canned logan
1 cup fruit cocktail
1 tbsp agar agar jelly powder
3 cups water
1 cup sugar
red, green and yellow food colouring
jackfruit syrup (see page 161)
crushed ice

### PREPARATION:

In a pot mix agar agar powder, sugar
and water. Bring to boil.
Divide boiled mixture into 3 portions and add
to each 1/8 teasp of different food colouring.
Place logan in individal
aluminium foil cups.
Fill with coloured jelly and let set.
Once coloured logan jelly sets, serve with
jackfruit syrup, fruit cocktatil and crushed ice.
Serve immediately.

### SERVES 4.

# JACKFRUIT SYRUP

### INGREDIENTS:

3 cups sugar
3 cups water
1 cup canned jackfruit, cut into strips

### PREPARATION:

Boil sugar and water in a small pot till sugar
dissolves. Add in jackfruit stirps
and remove from stove

# KHAO PHOT PING
### GRILLED CORN DESSERT

### INGREDIENTS:

1/4 cup mung bean flour
1/2 cup sugar

1/4 cup thick coconut milk
1  tsp salt
2  cups shaved fresh corn
1/4 cup desiccated coconut
2  pieces banana leaves of 5"x5"squares
butter for brushing

### PREPARATION:

In a pot, mix mung bean flour, sugar, coconut
milk and salt together. Bring to boil over
medium heat, stirring all the time with a
wooden spoon till mixture thickens.
Add in shaved corn and desiccated coconut.
Stir till well mixed
Remove from stove.
Brush banana leaves with butter and spoon 2
tbsp of corn mixture onto banana leaves and roll
into a rod. Seal both ends with
wooden tooth picks.
Grill banana parcels until fragrant and slightly
crisp on the outside.

### SERVES 4.

## PHONLAMAI NAM CHEUAM
### MIXED MELONS IN SYRUP

### INGREDIENTS;
1  cup scooped watermelon balls
1  cup scooped cantaloupe balls
1  cup scooped honeydew melon balls
2  cups jackfruit syrup (pg.161)
crushed ice

### PREPARATION;
Mix watermelon, cantaloupe and honeydew
melon balls with syrup in a  mixing bowl
and add in crushed ice.
Serve immediately.

**SERVES 4.**

## CANTALOUPE SA-KHU NAM CHEUAM KA-TI
### CANTALOUPE WITH SAGO PELLETS IN COCONUT MILK DESSERT

### INGREDIENTS:
1  cup sago or tapioca pellets, small
1  cup scooped cantaloupe balls
1/2  cup evaporated milk
2 1/2  cups thick coconut milk
2  cups palm sugar
1  tsp salt
crushed ice

### PREPARATION:
Prepare a pot of boiling water and add in sago
pellets. Boil until water becomes starchy.
Remove from stove and  wash off starch.
Boil sago pellets again
until they turn clear.
Drain and wash with water and soak till cool.
Drain and set aside for later use.
Mix evaporated milk, thick coconut milk, palm
sugar and salt together in a small pot.
Simmer over low heat stirring all the time
with a wooden spoon until mixture boils.
Serve cooked sago, melon balls
and coconut mixture with crushed ice.

**SERVES 4.**

## NOM-KROK SANKAYA
### EARTHEN BAKED CUSTARD

### INGREDIENTS:
1  cup eggs
1  cup palm sugar
1  cup thick coconut milk
2  tbsp corn flour
1/4  tsp vanilla extract
foi thong (see below) and lotus seeds for topping
Butter for brushing

### PREPARATION:
In a bowl, mix eggs, palm sugar, thick coconut milk,
vanilla extract and corn flour together.
Heat mixture in a double boiler over moderate heat
until sugar disolves and
mixture slightly thickens.
Strain mixture.
Brush nom-krok earthen pan with butter.
Heat earthen pan over direct heat until hot.
Pour mixture into hot depressions and bake over direct
heat till custard sets.
Top with foi thong and lotus seeds.
Remove custard and serve hot.

### FOI THONG
1 cup sugar
1 cup water
6 egg yolks, lightly beaten
Mix sugar and water together and boil until sugar
dissolves and mixture is syrupy. Using a cone with a
fine hole slowly drizzle egg yolks in a circular into
syrup. In 2-3 mins strands will have set and can be
gently removed with a fork or chopsticks.
Use as required.
**SERVES 4.**

163

# PHIAK SAGU RUAM-MIT
## SAGO DESSERT

### INGREDIENTS:

1 cup cooked big sago pellets (see page 163)
1/2 cup canned jackfruit, cut into strips
1 cup canned toddy palm seeds, sliced
1/2 cup canned water chestnuts, dice into cubes
3 cups thick coconut milk
1 1/2 cups tapioca flour
1 cup boiling water
1 tsp salt
1/4 tsp vanilla extract

### PREPARATION:

Dilute tapioca flour with water.
Divide cooked sago pellets into 2 portions and soak
with red and green syrup to get coloured sago.
Mix thick coconut milk, sugar, salt and vanilla extract
together in a pot and bring to boil, stirring all the time.
Once mixture boils, add in diluted tapioca flour mixture
and stir with wooden spoon till thick.
Add in coloured sago, jackfruit, toddy palm, water chestnuts
and stir till well mixed, Remove from stove and serve hot,

### SERVES 6.

# KHAO NIAO WAT
## GLUTINOUS PUMPKIN RICE

### INGREDIENTS:

2 cups glutinous rice
2 cups cooked pumpkin, diced
2 cups freshly grated coconut
1/4 cup ground roasted black
and white sesame seeds
1 cup sugar
1 tsp salt

### PREPARATION:

Wash glutinous rice and soak overnight.
Wash glutinous rice again. Steam rice in a piece of
muslin cloth in a steamer at high heat
until cooked, about 1/2 hour.
With a wooden spoon, mix cooked glutinous
rice and diced pumpkin together.
Press into fancy cups.
Mix ground sesame seeds with sugar and salt.
Steam freshly grated coconut shreds
over high heat for 5 mins
to prevent it from getting stale.
Arrange pumpkin rice on a serving plate.
Top with coconut shreds and sesame sugar.

### SERVES 4.

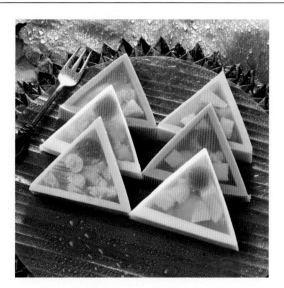

# WOON PHONLAMAI SAM-LIEAM
## TRIANGLE FRUIT JELLY

### (1) FRUIT JELLY INGREDIENTS:

1 tbsp agar agar jelly powder
3/4 cup sugar
3 cups water
2 cups fruit cocktail

### (2) COCONUT JELLY INGREDIENTS:

1 tbsp agar agar jelly powder
2 cups thick coconut milk
1 cup water
3/4 cup sugar
red and green food colouring

### PREPARATION:

Obtain 2 triangular aluminium trays, 3" width and 3" height.
Mix ingredients (1), except fruit cocktail in a pot and bring
to boil. Once mixture cooks, add fruit cocktail.
Pour jelly mixture into aluminium trays to 3/4 full.
Let set, about 1 hour.
Once fruit jelly sets, remove from tins.

Bring ingredients in (2) except colourings to boil.
Once mixture boils, divide into 2 portions.
Add 1/8 tsp of different colourings to each portions.
Pour coloured coconut jelly into empty
triangular tins till 1/2 full.
Immediately, immerse set fruit jelly into the centre of
liquid coconut jelly and cover with more coloured jelly.
Let it set before refrigerating.
Slice into pieces.
Serve cold.

### SERVES 8.

# ESSENTIAL BASICS

## Thai Flavours and Seasonings

Anyone who first experiences Thai Food may consider that it has only three tastes; hot, hotter and hottest. True connoisseurs would add that it also possesses an infinite variety of other flavours, both assertive and subtle, which collectively make it one of the most distinctive cuisines in Asia.

Culinary influences from countries such as China, India and even far-off Portugal have influenced Thai cooking over the centuries, bringing with them certain spices, herbs and other ingredients. The imported dishes underwent gradual alterations to accommodate Thai tastes, adopting to the local cuisine and ultimately becoming something uniquely Thai.

The explanation for the wide range of tastes are in the various combinations of the extraordinary array of herbs, spices and other ingredients that Thai cooks regard as essential. Some are bought from the nearest market but many can be picked fresh from your own kitchen garden. Undoubtedly, the most celebrated are the chillies which are not limited to just one or two varieties. We have dozens of scarcely distinguishable different kinds which vary in both flavour and potency. The most explosive is the smallest type called "*Phrik Khi Nu*" (which, translated literally, means "rat droppings" the name deriving from its shape). An encounter with one of those half-inch bombshells can make even a strong man dash for the nearest glass of water. A number of larger chillies which are several degrees milder, are also used for a less aggressive flavour. However, the pungent taste of Phrik Khi Nu is something thai food needs in every meal.

Equally important ingredients are aromatic leaves such as the coriander Plant *(Phak Chi,* cilantro) which is sprinkled lavishly on just about everything from soups to curries. Pandan or Screwpine *(Toei)* is an essential plant for Thai desserts. Its fresh leaves are much sought after for their unique fragrance and flavour which has no substitute, it is also used as a natural colouring extract for sweets.

Numerous other fresh plants are also added to Thai food for flavouring purposes such as lemongrass *(takhrai)* which lends a delicate aromatic citron taste or the leaves of kaffir lime *(bai makrut)* which are used for a similar purpose. For a long time, these two ingredients as well as other basic Thai seasonings were virtually unobtainable in Western countries. Countless travellers had to carry them as a souvenir for their homesick friends and relatives living abroad. Nowadays, thanks to the growing popularity of Thai restaurants, they can frequently be found in specialty markets in many of the world's major cities.

Several roots play a part in Thai cooking as well, either as an ingredient or as one of the numerous condiments that accompany every meal: for example, ginger (*khing*), galanga (*kha*) tumeric (*khamin*) and coriander roots.

Different parts of plants used in Thai cooking serve another purpose apart from their flavours. They are also highly regarded for their medicinal qualities.

Various fruits and vegetables are used to enhance the taste of Thai food. For a sour taste, lime juice is a must in Thai-style salads, another option for a milder and more subtle sour taste is tamarind (*makham*). Many recipes require this distinctive sour taste.

Another equally essential ingredient is coconut (*maphrao*). Coconut milk is used in both curries and sweets. The grated meat is a frequent addition to Thai desserts. Coconut sugar made from coconut nectar is preferred by most Thai cooks, especially in desserts.

Some special utensils are necessary tools in Thai cooking. Grating coconut flesh in order to make coconut milk requires an important tool called a "Kratai" which was wisely invented for this specific purpose. The unique aroma from cooking in an earthen pot is something that cannot be replaced by any other cooking utensils.

The proper combination of all these ingredients is regarded as an exclusive part of

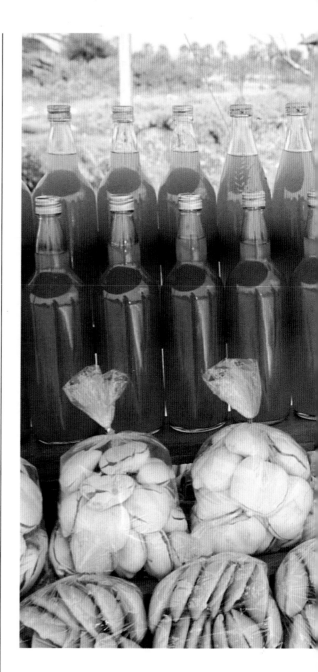

Thai food, one that requires both skill and time. A single specialty can take hours of grinding, tasting and delicate adjustments until the exact balance of flavours is acheived. Only then, according to masters of the art, can the true glory of Thai cooking be fully appreciated.

Thai food is currently enjoying an increasing international reputation. There are hundreds of Thai restaurants worldwide, in

almost every major city in the world. Thai cuisine has been discovered by innumerable food magazines and many articles have been written in praise of its exotic flavours.

The brief introduction of some of the main ingredients in Thai cuisine presented in this book should give the reader access to the exotic realm of Thai culinary art. Enjoy the cooking and discover one of the exclusive cuisines of Asia.

## Palm Sugar

Coconut nectar is not only consumed as a beverage but it can be processed into coconut sugar or palm sugar. The nectar after collection is gradually simmered till the liquid is condensed. Normally 5 litres of nectar will produce about 1 kg of palm sugar.

Thai cuisine prefers palm sugar to normal refined sugar as it gives a unique and aromatic taste and flavour plus its nutritional value is higher than processed sugar.

# KLUAI NAM WA CHEUAM
## CANDIED BANANAS

### INGREDIENTS:

14  kluai nam wa bananas, small
2  cups palm sugar
2 1/2  cups water

### PREPARATION:

Peel bananas and cut into 4 sections.
Soak cut bananas in lime solution (see page 201)
for 10 mins and drain.
In a pot or copper pan, mix sugar
and water together and bring to boil.
Add in bananas, turning now and then with a
wooden spoon. Cook over medium heat until
syrup thickens, banana pieces turn red
and syrup  has penetrated into bananas.

### SERVES 4.

# PHEUK/MAN CHEUAM
## CANDIED TARO/SWEET POTATOES

### INGREDIENTS:

3  lbs taro root or sweet potatoes
2  cups palm sugar
4  cups water

### PREPARATION:

Wash and peel taro root or sweet potatoes.
Cut into thick pieces.
Mix palm sugar and water in a pot
or copper pan and bring to a boil.
Add taro root or sweet potatoes to boiling syrup
turning now and then with a wooden spoon.
Cook over medium heat till syrup thickens
and has penetrated into
taro or sweet potatoe pieces.

### SERVES 4.

# CHILLIES

It is believed that chillies were discovered by Spanish explorers around the 14th Century in the New World regions i.e. Central America, South America and the West Indies Islands. Later in the 15th Century, chillie plantations spread to almost every European country, tropical America, Asia and India.

Chillies are classified in the Salunaceae strain. The Capsicum group has more than 100 different species. Chillies are short-lived crops and prefer loose and fertile soil. Some kinds have only a one-year lifetime while some may live for many years. Chillie seeds are planted and bear flowers around 2-3 months after being planted. They need lots of sunshine while bearing fruit.

Chillies vary in size from 1/2 inch to more than 11 inches. Some kinds of chillies are not so hot but some can be very hot, depending on the quantity of capsicine each contains. Chillies have beautiful colours ranging from white, ivory, yellow, orange, light green, and dark green to red, however, most will become red when ripe.

Europeans classify chillies as an herb because of its medicinal qualities. Chillies are also a good source of vitamins A, B1, B2 and C. In Asian countries where strong-tasting foods are prefered, chillies are used for flavouring and garnishing hot and savoury dishes and are classified as a spice. Chillies play such a remarkable role in Thai daily life that there is a saying, "those who do not know Namprik (Thai dipping/dressing), Kangped (Thai curry) or Yam (Thai salad) seasoned by chillies will never get the real taste of food".

Thai people have been using chillies for a long time, mainly for cooking. Chillies can be grown in all kinds of soil, even sandy soil but do prefer hot weather and lots of rain. Nowadays chillies are widely grown in many countries and exported to the world market. The major producing and exporting countries are India, China, Pakistan, Indonesia, Mexico, Tanzania and Bangladesh. In Thailand, chillies are cultivated as a main and supplement crop in many provinces such as Ratchaburi, Utradit, Petchburi, Kanjanaburi, and Prachuabkirikhan. The total production volume is approximately 100,000 metric tons per year. However, some years the demand for local use is so high that a considerable amount of chillies have to be imported from abroad.

Chillies that are widely cultivated are mostly local species such as Khee Chilli, Chee Fah Chilli, Yellow Chilli, Jinda Chilli or Giant Chilli. They are grown on large-size plantations for easy watering and gathering. For commercial purpose, chillies are separated into small and large sizes. Formerly, farmers mainly cultivated and sold fresh chillies, but lately the local demand for dried chillies is gradually increasing. Farmers now grow both small and large chillies most of which are for the dried chilli market. Dried chillies are exported, both ground and whole. Major markets are Japan, Germany and Singapore.

**Pepper** is a branching, perennial climbing plant. The leaves are green and ovate. Flowers are minute, in spikes. The fruit is small, round and green in colour, turning to bright red when ripe. Pepper is cultivated on a large scale in eastern Thailand as well as in some southern provinces.

Fresh pepper contains 63.4% water, 4.8% protein, 27.3% carbohydrates, and 2.7% fat. It has 153 Calories/100g. Pepper contains iron, calcium, phosphorus, vitamin A, and niacin. Dried pepper contains 12.9% water, 11.5% protein, 49.5% carbohydrates, 6.8% fat, and 14.9% fiber. It has 305 Calories/100g. It also contains iron, calcium, phosphorus and more niacin but no vitamin A is found.

The strong and pungent smell of pepper is from Piperine, the main chemical substance found in pepper. Pepper contains about 4.5%-8% piperine which accounts for its unique aroma. This pungent and aromactic spice is used as an ingredient in many kinds of herbal medicine.

During the reign of King Ramatibodi III of Ayudhya Period, chillies from South America travelled to Spain. The Spanish developed a taste for this newly discovered exotic spice. They expanded their chilli plantations and introduced this new taste to England and the European continent.

Later, Spanish and Portugese traders brought chillies to Asia. India, a country rich in culinary art, started cooking spicy food and this new food culture spread to China. Thai people became familiar with the hot taste only 300 years ago. Before the introduction of chillies into Thai cuisine, Thai food must have been very bland. Before the introduction of chillies the only two seasonings available were salt and pepper.

Besides seasoning savoury dishes with fresh and dried chillies and pepper, Thai people also use chilli sauce. Chilli sauce goes well with seafood as well as other main dishes. The main ingredients of chilli sauce are garlic, sugar, vinegar, salt and chillies.

Chillies that are suitable for producing chilli sauce should be red, either fresh or dried. The degree of hotness can be adjusted to extremely hot, medium or mild during preparation. The fully ripe Yellow chillies are also good for making chilli sauce.

## The Difference Between Red Curry Paste and Green Curry Paste

Thai people have various styles of cooking; boiled, stirred fried, fried or "kaeng" (a typical Thai-style cooking). Popular dishes included in every meal either in the daily menu, family gatherings, informal parties or special occasions are called *"Kaeng Phed"*.

Kaeng Phed is made by dissolving curry paste with coconut milk or plain water, adding meat, vegetables and seasonings. Mixed with plain water it is called Kaeng Pa. The type mixed with coconut milk is divided into 2 groups. The one using red dried chillies is known as "Kaeng Phed" the other using fresh green chillies is known as "Kaeng Keow Wan"

The difference between these two curry pastes are as follows : Kaeng Phed curry paste or red curry paste consists of coriander seeds (*Lak Phak Chi*), cumin seeds (*Yira*), dried chillies (*Phrik Haeng*), salt, galanga (*Kha*), lemongrass (*Takhrai*), dried skin of kaffir lime (*Piew Makrut*), coriander root (*Rak Phak Chi*) , pepper corn (*Phrik Thai Med*), shallots (*Huahom Daeng*), garlic (*krathiam*) and shrimp paste (*Kapi*). Kaeng Keow Wan curry paste or green curry paste consists of *Phrik Khi Nu* (fresh small green chillies), salt, galanga (*Kha*), lemongrass (*Takhrai*), dried skin of kaffir lime (*Piew Makrut*), whole coriander plant (leaves and root), pepper corns (*Phrikthai Med*), shallots (*Huahom Daeng*) garlic (*Krathiam*) and shrimp paste (*Kapi*).

Other important ingredients which cannot be omitted are coconut milk, meat, vegetables i.e. miniature eggplants (*Makhua Phuang*), young round eggplants (*Makhua On*), green eggplants (*Makhua Yao* and aromatic vegetables i.e. kaffir lime leaves (*Bai Makrut*) and sweet basil (*bai Horapha*).

## NAM PHRIK KAPI
### SHRIMP CHILLI PASTE

### INGREDIENTS:

1 tbsp roasted shrimp paste
1 tbsp fried dried prawns
2 tbsp shallots, sliced
10 hot chillies
2 tbsp lime juice
2 tbsp palm sugar
1 tbsp fish sauce

### PRAPARATION:

Mix grilled shrimp paste and shallots
in a mortar and pound to a fine paste.
Add in dried prawns and chillies
and pound till well mixed.

Mix ground paste with lime juice,
palm sugar and fish sauce.

## KAENG KEOW WAN THALAY
### SEAFOOD IN GREEN CURRY

### INGREDIENTS:

1/4 cup white fish fillets
1/4 cup cleaned and scored squid pieces
1/4 cup cleaned and shelled prawns
1 cup green eggplant, cut and soak in water
1/4 cup green curry paste
3 cups thick coconut milk
2 tbsp vegetable oil
2 tbsp palm sugar
2 tbsp fish sauce
sweet basil leaves,
red and green chilli strips for garnish

### PREPARATION:

In a medium pot, with 2 tbsp vegetable oil, fry
green curry paste until fragrant.
Mix in fish fillets, squid and prawns.
Add coconut milk and simmer for 10 mins.
Season with palm sugar and fish sauce.
Add drained, soaked eggplant
and bring curry to boil again.
Top with sweet basil and chillies.
Serve over steamed rice.

### SERVES 4.

# KAENG PHRIK SOT KAP KAI
## CHICKEN CURRY WITH FRESH CHILLIES

### INGREDIENTS:

4 cups thick coconut milk
1 cup red and green chillies, de-seed and slice
5 slices galangal
2 5" pieces lemon grass, smashed
5 kaffir lime leaves, torn
2 cups chicken breast, diced into cubes
2 tbsp fish sauce
2 tbsp palm sugar
sweet basil leaves for topping

### PREPARATION:

In a medium pot heat thick coconut milk
over medium heat. Add galangal,
lemon grass, and kaffir lime leaves.
Once mixture boils, add chillies and chicken.
Simmer until chicken is cooked. Season with fish
sauce and palm sugar. Let mixture boil again for
5 mins and remove from stove.
Top with sweet basil leaves and serve.

### SERVES 4.

# NAM PHRA PHRIK
## CHILLIES WITH FISH SAUCE

### INGREDIENTS:

10 hot chillies (finely sliced)
5 garlic gloves, sliced
3 tbsp fish sauce
1 tbsp lime juice

### PREPARTION:

Mix above ingredients together and serve.
Usually, this sauce is served with
cooked rice and clear soups.

# TAO JIAO LON
## SPICY FERMENTED SOY BEAN DIP

### INGREDIENTS:

1 1/2 cups thick coconut milk
1/4 cup , fermented white soybeans (tao jiao)
coarsely ground
1/2 cup minced pork
1/2 cup minced prawns
3 tbsp shallots, sliced
8 red and green chillies, de-seed and slice
1/4 tsp salt
3 tbsp palm sugar
3 tbsp tamarind juice

### PREPARATION:

Place coconut milk in a wok and
boil until oil seeps out, stirring all the time.
Add tao jiao (fermented white soybeans),
minced pork and prawns.
Cook until mixture boils.
Add shallots and chillies.
Season with salt, palm sugar
and tamarind juice.
Bring mixture to boil and remove from stove.
Serve with fresh vegetables,
fluffy fried cat fish or cooked mackerel.

### SERVES 4.

## NAM PHRIK KAENG KEOW WAN
### GREEN CHILLI CURRY PASTE

### INGREDIENTS:

1 tbsp coriander seeds
1/4 tsp cumin seeds
20 hot green chillies, cut into pieces
3 yellow chillies, cut into pieces
1 tsp salt
1 tbsp galangal, chopped
1 tbsp lemon grass, sliced
1/2 tsp rind of kaffir lime
3 tbsp chopped whole coriander plant
1/4 tsp pepper corns
2 tbsp shallots, sliced
1/4 cup garlic, sliced
1 tsp roasted shrimp paste

### PREPARATION:

In a shallow pan, dry fry coriander seeds
and cumin seeds until fragrant.
After seeds are cool grind into a powder.
Place green and yelow chillies, salt, galangal,
lemon grass, kaffir lime rind, chopped
coriander plant (cilantro), pepper corns, shallots,
garlic and shrimp paste in a blender and
grind until a fine paste is formed.
Mix the curry paste with the powdered seed
mixture. Fill a wok with 3 tbsp vegetable oil and
fry the spice mixture over low heat until fragrant.
Cool and keep refrigerated
in an air-tight container.
Can be used for a period of 3 months.

## NAM PHRIK GAENG PHET
### RED CHILLI CURRY PASTE

### INGREDIENTS:

2 tsp coriander seeds
1 tsp cumin seeds
7 dried chillies
1 tsp salt
1 tsp galangal
2 tbsp lemon grass, sliced
2 tsp rind of kaffir lime

1 tbsp coriander root, chopped
1/4 tsp pepper corns
3 tbsp shallots, sliced
1/4 cup garlic, sliced
1 tsp roasted shrimp pasted

### PREPARATION:
In a shallow pan, dry fry coriander seeds
and cumin seeds till fragrant.
Cool and grind to powder.
Remove seeds from dry chillies and soak in hot
water for 1/2 hour. Squeeze dry and place in a
blender with salt, galangal, lemon grass,
kaffir lime rind, coriander root, pepper corns,
shallots, garlic and shrimp paste. Blend till
mixture forms a smooth paste.
With 3 tbsp vegetable oil, fry curry mixture over
low heat until fragrant. Cool and seal in
a jar to be kept in the refrigerator.
Can be used for 3 months.

## NAM PHRIK KAENG KRUA
### MILDER RED CHILLI PASTE

### INGREDIENTS:

5 dried red chillies
1 tsp salt
1 tsp galangal
1 tbsp lemon grass
1/2 tsp rind of kaffir lime
1/4 tsp pepper corns
1 tbsp coriander root, chopped
2 tbsp shallots, sliced
3 tbsp garlic, sliced
1 tsp roasted shrimp paste

### PREPAPATION:

Remove seeds from dried chillies and
soak in hot water for 1/2 hr.
Drain and squeeze dry.
Mix chillies, salt, galangal, lemon grass, kaffir
lime rind, pepper corns, coriander root,
shallots, garlic and shrimp paste in
a blender and grind to a fine paste.
In a wok, with 3 tbsp vegetable oil, fry curry
paste over low heat until fragrant. Cool and keep
sealed in a jar. Can be refrigerated
for a period of 3 months.
This is a milder curry paste and is normally used
in sweet and sour sauces or curries.

# NAM PHRIK PHAO
## ROASTED CHILLI PASTE

### INGREDIENTS:

20  dried red chillies, deep-fried
10  dried hot chillies, deep-fried
1  cup garlic, sliced and fried
1/2  cup shallots, sliced and fried
1/4  cup tamarind juice
1  tbsp roasted shrimp paste
1/4  cup palm sugar
2  tbsp fish sauce
1/4  cup dried shrimps, fried and ground
1/2  cup vegetable oil

### PREPARATION:

In a food processor, mix dried chillies, hot chillies, garlic, shallots,
shrimp paste and dried shrimps together
and grind to a fine paste.
In a wok, with vegetable oil, fry ground
chilli paste over low heat until fragrant.
Add palm sugar, tamarind juice and fish sauce. Cook, stirring
constantly until well mixed or until oil seeps to the surface.
Cool and place in sealed jars. Can be kept in the
refrigerator for a period of 3 months.
Normally used in tom yam soup or fried with seafood.

189

## PHRA KAPONG
## PHAT PHRIK KHING
**RED SNAPPER WITH MILDER RED CURRY PASTE**

### INGREDIENTS:

2 cups sliced white fish fillets
1/2 cup milder red curry paste (page 187)
3 yellow and green chillies, de-seed and slice
4 tbsp palm sugar
2 tbsp fish sauce
5 kaffir lime leaves, shredded
vegetable oil for frying

### PREPARATION:

Rub fish fillets with a dash of salt
and pepper and deep-fry
in a wok of hot oil till crisp. Drain.
With 3 tbsp vegetable oil in a wok
fry chilli paste till fragrant.
Add palm sugar, fish sauce and chillies.
Add crisp fish fillets
and carefully fry till well mixed.
Remove from wok and serve topped with
kaffir lime shreds.

### SERVES 4.

## TOD MUN PHRA
### FISH CAKES

### INGREDIENTS:

2 cups fresh white fish
1 cup yard long beans, finely sliced
5 kaffir lime leaves, shredded
1/4 cup red chilli curry paste
1 egg
2 tbsp fish sauce
1 tbsp sugar
vegetable oil for deep fryng

### PREPARATION:

Using a cleaver mince fish into a smooth paste.
Beat minced fish in mixing bowl until firm.
Add in red chilli curry paste, egg,
fish sauce and sugar.
Beat till well mixed.
Mix in yard long beans and
kaffir lime leaf shreds.

Prepare a pan of hot oil.
With wet fingers scoop and flatten fish mixture
into individual cakes.
Drop flattened fish cakes
into hot oil for frying.
Deep-fry fish cakes until cooked.
Serve with cucumber relish. See page 35.

### SERVES 4.

# EARTHEN POT

In olden days, the earthen pot played a vital role in Thai daily life. It was used as a rice cooker, frying pan, boiling pot or whatever you could think of. Its popularity was probably due to the unique aromatic fragrance imparted after cooking. No other cooking container can compete with an earthen pot. Certain Thai specialities, such as shrimp or crab baking, specifically require an eathen pot for cooking.

In the rural countryside, earthen pots, the sizes of which vary, are still greatly valued for holding drinking water. The earthen pot is exceptionally useful in the summer when the heat is very strong. Water kept inside these large clay pots

stays cool and refreshing through the long, hot summer months.

For medical purposes, traditional doctors use the earthen pot as the utensil to brew medicine called "Ya Mor" (pot medicine). One batch of this boiled and re-boiled herbal concoction can last until the dosage becomes tasteless. Sometimes, the doctor will heat the pot containing medicinal salt and massage the patient with it.

# KAENG SOM MOR-DIN
### SPICY SOUR TAMARIND SOUP
### WITH VEGETABLES

## PRAWN CHILLI PASTE INGREDIENTS:

7 dried chillies
1/2 tsp salt
2 tbsp garlic, sliced
1/4 cup shallots, sliced
1 tsp roasted shrimp paste
1/2 cup cooked prawns

### PREPARATION:

Remove seeds from chillies and soak in
hot water for 1/2 hour.
Drain and squeeze dry.
In a blender, mix dried chillies, salt, garlic,
shallots, shrimp paste
and cooked prawns together
and blend to a fine paste.

## OTHER INGREDIENTS:

1/2 cup cleaned and shelled prawns
1/2 cup sliced carrots
1/2 cup cabbage, cut into pieces
1/4 cup yard long beans, cut to 1" strips
1/4 cup Chinese cabbage, cut into pieces
4 tbsp tamarind juice
2 tbsp palm sugar
2 tbsp fish sauce
4 cups chicken stock
the above prawn chilli paste

### PREPARATION:

In an earthen pot, bring stock to boil and add in
prawn chilli paste. Simmer for 10 mins before
adding shelled prawns, carrots, cabbage,
yard long beans, Chinese cabbage
and tamarind juice.
Season with palm sugar and fish sauce.
Let simmer till cooked.
Serve hot.

### SERVES 4.

# COCONUT AND COCONUT NECTAR

Coconut is a perennial plant usually grown along seasides. The whole tree is an invaluable commodity in our Thai society. The trunk and leaves are used in building and shading, whereas the fruits can be consumed young or fully ripe.

The shells in the old days were used as ladles for water or bowls for food. The older kernels are grated and compressed to make coconut milk and boiled to get coconut oil. The sun-dried, compressed and grated coconut known as copra, can be used as a fertilizer or animal feed.

The husk are used as filler in cushions, beds or stuffed chairs. Sun-dried to ash form it is used in our phiak poon dessert. Dried husks also make an excellent mulch in the growing of orchids. Its endless usage is remarkable.

The sweet refreshing young coconut water is a treat all year round. The older generation of Thais believe it has cleansing and cooling properties. Daily consumption of young coconut water during the last days of pregnancy will cool the heat from the body.

THE VEGETARIAN TASTE
OF THAILAND

The coconut water found inside the kernel is different from coconut milk. Coconut milk is the compressed liquid from the flesh of older coconuts. Coconut milk is an important ingredient in our Thai lifestyle, and is used in our daily cooking and for Thai desserts.

The process of making coconut milk begins with the removal of the kernel. A kratia, or rabbit grater invented by our ancestors is used to grate the meat. Finally the grated coconut is pressed through a muslin cloth to extract the concentrated milk. The rich and flavourish taste of coconut milk is an indispensible ingredient in our cuisine.

198

Besides coconut water and coconut milk, there is yet another kind of beverage that we can get from the coconut; coconut nectar.

Coconut nectar is extracted from the coconut flower spikes. The tips of the spikes are partially cut and gently bent down to slowly drip into a bamboo container. The flower spikes drip for a period of 10 to 12 hrs.

Usually one coconut tree can bear 2 to 4 spikes at a time producing about 1 to 2 litres of nectar per day. After boiling, the coconut nectar is ready for drinking. The drink is a refreshing treat served with crushed ice.

199

# AISA-KHRIM KA-THI
## YOUNG COCONUT ICE CREAM

### INGREDIENTS:

1 young coconut, spoon flesh and cut into pieces
3 cups thick coconut milk
1 cup evaporated milk
2 cups sugar
2 tsp salt
3 tbsp corn flour

### PREPARATION:

In a pot, mix corn flour, evaporated milk
and sugar together. Simmer over low heat
until sugar dissolves and mixture thickens.
Add in coconut milk and stir till well mixed.
Strain mixture.
Cool mixture and mix in young coconut flesh.
Pour into an ice-cream machine.
Crank until mixture stiffens,
about 45 mins to 1 hour.
Remove ice-cream from machine
Freeze for 2 hours before serving.

**SERVES 4.**

# KA-NOM TOM KAO
## BOILED STUFFED COCONUT BALLS

### FLOUR INGREDIENTS:
2 cups glutinous rice flour
3/4 cup water

### PREPARATION:
Mix the above together and knead in a mixing
bowl till soft. Cover with a piece
of wet cloth for later use.

### COCONUT FILLING
2 cups grated coconut
1 cup palm sugar
1 cup water

### PREPARATION:
Mix coconut shreds, palm sugar and water
together. Boil until mixture dries out and
thickens to a sticky sustance.

Cool and roll coconut mixture into 1/2" marbles.
Roll rice flour mixture into 1" balls.
Forming a cavity with the little finger
fill rice flour balls with coconut marbles.
Seal tightly.
Drop coconut balls into boilingwater.
Boil until glutinous rice balls float.
Coat glutinous rice balls with more grated
coconut shreds and serve.

**SERVES 4.**

# KA-NOM PHIAK POON
## COCONUT RICE FLOUR CAKES

2 cups rice flour
2 tbsp sago flour
2 cups screwpine juice (see page 203)
1 3/4 cups palm sugar
1 grated coconut
5 cups lime solution (see below)

### PREPARATION:

To extract screwpine juice, clean 20 screwpine leaves
and finely chop. Blend with 2 cups of water in a food
processor until liquefied.
Strain screwpine juice and use as required.
With hand mix screwpine juice, lime solution, palm
sugar, rice flour and sago flour together until flour and
sugar dissolve into solution. Strain mixture.
Cook over medium heat, stirring with a wooden
spoon, until mixture bubbles and thickens.
Grease a 10"x10"x2" tray and pour batter
into greased tray to set.
Grate coconut into long shreds
and mix with 1 tsp salt.
Steam grated coconut over high heat for 5 minutes
to prevent it from getting stale.
Cut dessert into pieces and top with grated coconut.

### LIME SOLUTION
1/8 cup lime (calcium oxide)
6 cups water
Mix lime and water together ( a.k.a. calcium
hydroxide) and leave overnight. Strain and use only
clear solution as required.

For black phiak poon, mix 1/2 cup ground coconut
husk ash into mixture before cooking.

To prepare coconut husks sun dry 2 coconut husks and
burn husk to ash in a container.
Pound mixture into a powder.
Use as required.

**SERVES 6.**

# SCREWPINE, PANDAN OR PANDANUS

A tropical erect shrub growing to 0.5 to 1 metre in height, the stem bearing a few prop-roots, the leaves are spirally crowded towards the inner bulb. Individual leaves are long, narrow, green and smooth with pointed tips.

In Malaysia, Singapore and Indonesia, this fragrant essential plant is known as pandan, derived from its scientific name pandanus and commonly known as screwpine.

Screwpine is grown abundantly near any water catchment areas, e.g ponds, lakes and backyards where the soil is usually moist, Flourishing easily after planting it does not need much tending given the required habitant.

Due to its shrub like form, screwpine is commonly grown as an ornamental plant for landscaping. It is often employed in perfect combination in floral arrangements.

Looking at any Thai menu, screwpine usage appears in many forms. Fresh leaves containing an aromatic oil, which is cardiotonic, is either cut and pounded in a mortar or shredded to be blended in a liquidizer with some water to extract the greenish aromatic flavouring extract required in the many Thai desserts. It is essential for the famous green pandan chiffon cakes found in Asian countries.

Besides colouring and flavoring, screwpine also adds a refreshing aromatic taste to food and desserts. Dried leaves are often used as one of the ingredients in many herbal teas. Screwpine leaves, brewed in chinese teas make a refreshing thirst quencher. Cooked with rice or porridge, as a wraper for savoury food, in desserts, or as a flavour or colouring, its abundant usage is something we Thais can never forgo for another replacement. Its place in our culture and lifestyle for hundreds of years is still growing strong.

# KAI HOR BAI TOEY
## CHICKEN WRAPPED IN SCREWPINE PARCELS

### INGREDIENTS:
20 chicken fillets of 2"x 2" pieces
20 big screwpine leaves, cut into 6" pieces
4 tbsp sesame seeds, roasted and ground
1 tbsp sesame oil
1 tbsp garlic, chopped
1 tbsp coriander root, chopped
1 tsp ground pepper
2 tbsp oyster sauce
2 tbsp Maggi sauce
1 tbsp sugar
wooden tooth picks for securing parcels
vegetable oil for frying

### PREPARATION:
In a mortar, grind garlic
and coriander root together.
Mix chicken pieces with ground spices, ground
sesame seeds, sesame oil, oyster sauce,
Maggi sauce, sugar and pepper.
Marinate for 1 hour. Wrap chicken with
screwpine leaves and secure with tooth picks.
Prepare a wok with hot oil and fry screwpine
chicken parcels over high heat
till crisp or until they float.
Drain and serve with sauce.

### SAUCE
### INGREDIENTS:
1/4 cup soy sauce
2 tsp black soy sauce
1/4 cup palm sugar
1 tsps sesame oil
1 tbsp roasted ground sesame seeds

### PREPARATION:
Mix all above ingredients, except roasted ground
sesame seeds, in a pot and bring
to a boil over medium heat.
Once mixture boils add sesame seeds and
remove from heat.
Serve with fried screwpine chicken.

### SERVES 10.

# NAM KA-TI
## COCONUT MILK DESSERT SAUCE

### INGREDIENTS:

4 cups thick coconut milk
2 cups palm sugar
2 tsp salt
4 screwpine leaves, knotted

### PREPARATION:

In a pot, mix coconut milk, palm sugar, salt
and screwpine leaves.
Simmer coconut mixture over low heat,
stirring with a wooden spoon all the time
to prevent it from burning.
Cook till sugar dissolves. Remove from stove
when mixture starts to boil.
Cool and serve with desserts.

# TAMARIND

A large spreading evergreen tree with feathery compound leaves. The flowers are in lateral racements and are yellow with red stripes. The pods are long and slightly curved, plump and cinnamon brown in colour when fully ripe. They contain a soft brownish pulp which gives an agreeably acidic taste.

The pulp contains 12-15 percent organic acids including tartaric and citric acids. The tamarind pulp is a main ingredient in Thai food, its unique sour taste is something irreplaceable. Besides the pulp of the tamarind pod, some particular Thai dishes are garnished with the pleasantly sour tasting young tamarind leaves.

The pods of sweet tamarind when fully ripe are not used for cooking. They are eaten fresh. The taste is sweet and mildly sour.

Apart from its culinary characteristics, the tamarind pulp is also used as a laxative in traditional Thai medicine. The kernels from roasted ripe seed pods are used as an anthelmintic for threadworms in children.

For household use, the tamarind pulp mixed with water can be used to clean the copperware and brassware very well.

# NAM MA-KHAM
## REFRESHING TAMARIND DRINK

### INGREDIENTS:

1 cup tamarind pulp
8 cups hot water
3 cups sugar
2 tsp salt

### PREPARATION:

Mix tamarind pulp with hot water
for about 15 mins.
Squeeze and strain tamarind extract.
In a pot, mix sugar, salt and tamarind extract
together and let mixture simmer
until sugar dissolves.
Cool and serve with crushed ice.

**SERVES 4.**

# MA-KHAM KIAO
## TAMARIND SWEETS

### INGREDIENTS:

2 1/2 cups tamarind pulp
2 cups sugar
1 tbsp hot chillies, de-seed and grind
2 tsp salt
1/2 cup water
sugar for coating

### PREPARATION:

Remove seeds from tamarind pulp.
Mix sugar, salt, water, ground chillies and
tamarind pulp together in a copper pan.
Stirring with a wooden spoon
cook over low heat till thick and rollable.
Cool and roll mixture into 1/2" marbles.
Coat with sugar.
Keep in air-tight containers or wrap individually
with cellophane papers.

# NAM-PHRIK MA-KHAM PHIAK
## SPICY TAMARIND DIP

### INGREDIENTS:

1 cup cooked white fish
10 dried red chillies
1/2 cup shallots, sliced
1/2 cup chopped garlic
2 tsp chopped galangal
1 cup tamarind pulp, remove seeds and chop
1/4 cup palm sugar
2 tbsp fish sauce
1 tsp roasted shrimp paste
1/4 cup vegetable oil

### PREPARATION:

Remove seeds from chillies and
soak in hot water for 1/2 hour.
Cool and squeeze chillies dry.
Place chillies, salt, garlic, galangal, shallots and
shrimp paste in a food processor and blend till
mixture turns to a fine paste.
Add fish and tamarind pulp
and blend till well mixed.

In a frying pan with vegetable oil fry blended
ingredients over low heat till fragrant.
Add in fish sauce and palm sugar
and cook till well mixed.
Serve tamarind dip with fresh vegetables.

**SERVES 6.**

# GLUTEN

When cooking, some ingredients can be replaced with gluten leaving the delectable taste similar to the original recipe. For those who want to avoid eating meat but cannot yet stop the craving, gluten is a delicious substitute.

The use of protein from wheat flour instead of meat in cooking not only does the least harm to earth's living creatures, but also fills life with true mental and physical happiness.

Protein from wheat flour has been used for quite a long time although it was not so widely known. In Chinese wheat gluten is known as Mee Kng.

Gluten is made from wheat flour which has been washed till it transform into a soft, bouncy, brownish mass with a mild tofu-like aroma. Gluten is always shaped to imitate many kinds of meat, such as pork or meatballs. During the Vegetarian Festival, the vendors alway make it similar to animals such as chicken, duck, lobster or crab, depending on how far their imagination goes. These products are made ready to use and can be found in food markets. Chinese people in Thailand normally buy Gluten products from the markets in Chinatown.

Wheatflour is comprised of starch granules containing about 10-14% protein consisting of 4 differnt types of protein i.e. Albumin, Globolin, Gliadin and Glutentin. The first two types have no part in the process of gluten making since they are dissolved when mixed with water.

The other 2 types of protein, when mixed with water, will adhere and transform into a net-like form called Gluten.

Therefore, when blended together, gliadin will become paste-like while glutenin will form into strands; gliadin will gradually hold the glutenin strands together. The wheat flour has to be blended

with water for about 20 minutes, either by machine or hand, and rested for 30 minutes covered with a damp cloth to let the texture become firmer. After that, the gluten dough must be thoroughly rinsed with water to wash away the excess starch granules and set aside for another 1/2-1 hour before making it into the desired shapes. Gluten must be kept in a refregirator and re-boiled before using.

Gluten must be boiled in hot water, using medium heat in order to get a firm texture; high heat will create bubbles in the texture. While boiling, salt should be added to make Gluten taste better and have a more elastic texture.

Another kind of protein which is now favoured by many vegetarians in Thailand is Soya Protein made from soy flour. Soy beans are pressed, cooked, dehydrated and milled before being made into different sizes and shapes. The soya protein must be soaked into water until soft, hot water will soften it faster. Soya protein is then ready to be cooked as a meat substitute.

# MEE-KNG
## WASHING OF WHEAT GLUTEN

**INGREDIENTS:**

2 3/4  lbs bread flour
3  cup water
3  tbsp vegetable oil
1 tbsp salt

**PREPARATION:**

Mix flour and salt in mixer, add in water
and vegetable oil and knead till elastic
and smooth.
Rest dough for 1/2 hour.
Wash gluten in a basin and knead
and scrub gluten till it is an elastic mass
or till water is clear.
Relax gluten after washing for about 15 mins
then form shapes as required.
Bring a pot of water and salt to boil.
Cook gluten in salted water
for 10 mins or till it floats.
Drain and soak in cold water before using.

## WASHING OF WHEAT GLUTEN, STEP-BY-STEP

**1. Displaying of ingredients.**

**2. Mix flour and salt in a mixer.**

**3. Add in water and oil to flour mixture.**

**4. Knead to a smooth dough.**

**5. Rest mixed dough for 1/2 hour.**

**6. Washing of gluten mass.**

**7. The washed gluten mass.**

**8. Making gluten shapes.**

**9. Boiling the shaped gluten.**

**10. The finished product.**

# INDEX

# GLOSSARY

**Agar-Agar,** a thickening agent made from seaweed. Agar-agar is available in sheets of translucent strands or in a powder and can be found in most Asian markets and sometimes in health food stores.

**Basil.** There are many types of basil. The most commonly used basil in Thai cooking is sweet basil, *horapha.* It has deep green leaves and often reddish or purple stems. It has a taste reminiscent of anise and is especially good in curries. If you can not find *horapha* any basil can be substituted. *Maenglak* is another Thai sweet basil with light green leaves and a tangy taste.

**Bean Curd,** is made from soybeans that are soaked, ground, mixed with water and briefly cooked before being placed in a wooden mold to drain and solidify. There are several types of bean curd. Different types of dishes and different methods of cooking call for different types of bean curd. Soft white bean curd, *tau hoo,* is most often steamed or added to soups while the firm type, *tao kwa,* is used for stir-frying, deep frying and braising. Refrigerated bean curd will keep for about five days if the water is changed daily. Pressed and deep fried bean curd is also available. It can be found in dried cakes in most Asian markets.

**Bean Curd, fermented,** *tau hoo yee,* is more like cheese than tofu. It can be eaten with rice, used in cooking to enrich vegetable dishes or used as a seasoning. The two most common types are red fermented bean curd and white fermented bean curd. The red variety is cured in a brine with fermented red rice flavored with annatto seeds and rice wine.

**Bean Curd, spongy.** Deep-frying bean curd changes the texture into a sponge-like substance. This allows the bean curd to absorb the flavors of the sauce when it is cooked for a second time.

**Bean Sauce,** a seasoning made from fermented soybeans, flour and salt. This very popular Asian seasoning appears as yellow bean sauce, brown bean sauce, black bean sauce and hot bean sauce. The preferred sauce is made from whole beans as the ground varieties are often quite salty.

**Beans, black fermented,** also known as salted black beans are cooked and fermented with salt and spices. These small, black, salted soy beans have a fantastic flavor when combined with garlic, fresh ginger, or chilies. Some chefs soak the beans before use, others use directly from the container, crushing or chopping lightly to release the aroma.

**Cardamom,** *luk kra-wan, Amomum krevanh,* appear like miniature unhusked coconuts. The pods and seeds are used in both sweet and savory dishes, especially curries. For best results grind the seeds just before using.

**Celery,** *kheun chai, Apium graveolens,* also called celeriac, turniprooted celery or Chinese celery has very small stalks and a very strong flavor.

**Chicken stock,** *nam sup,* made from fresh chicken is preferred in Thai cooking. While plain water can be substituted and the instant chicken broth cubes and pastes are certainly fast and convenient, they do not compare to home made stock. Chop 3 1/2 pounds of chicken bones and scraps into 3-4 inch pieces and place in a stock pot with 10 cups of water and allow to stand for 30 minutes. Peel 1 Chinese radish, cut in half length-wise and add to pot. Wash 3 celery plants and 3 garlic plants and remove the roots of the celery plants. Coil the celery and garlic plants together, tie into a bundle and add to the pot together with 5 bay leaves and 1 tablespoon salt. Heat to boiling, simmer over low heat for 1-1 1/2 hours and then strain through cheesecloth.

**Chilies,** *phrik, Capsicum annum,* several varieties are available in Thailand. As they ripen they change color from green to red and become hotter. Removing the seeds and pulp from fresh chilies reduces their hotness.
Fully ripe fruits are dried in the sun to give dried chilies, *phrik haeng* and these are pounded for ground dried chili, *prik pon.*

**Chilies, hot,** *phrik khi nu,* are the hottest type and also the smallest, being only about a centimeter long. Generally the smaller the chili the hotter the flavor.

**Chili Sauce,** *phrik saus,* is made from water, chilies, salt, vinegar and sugar. The taste and degree of hotness or sweetness varies according to the brand. Many different brands from most Asian countries are available.

**Chili Paste,** *nam phrik phao,* see page 189

**Chinese Chives,** *ton kui chai,* Allium tuberosum, has fairly thick, narrow flat leaves which are eaten with fried noodle dishes such as Phat Thai.

**Cilantro** (see coriander)

**Coconut Milk**, *ka-thi* is the white liquid that is squeezed from grated coconut meat and not the juice inside the coconut. The use of coconut milk in curries is a hallmark of Thai cooking. To prepare about 1 1/2 cups coconut milk, add 2 cups fresh grated coconut to a food processor or blender. Add 1 1/4 cups very hot water and blend at high speed for one minute. Strain mixture through a fine sieve, pressing hard with a wooden spoon to extract as much liquid as possible. This is coconut milk. For recipes calling for thick coconut milk, allow the coconut milk to stand for a while, the thick milk will rise to the top. Spoon it off the top. The left over liquid will be light coconut milk. To prepare coconut milk from dried coconut flakes empty an 8-ounce package of unsweetened dried coconut flakes into a food processor. Add 1 7/8 cups of very hot, near boiling, water. Process with quick on and off pulses for 25 seconds or until well mixed. Strain the mixture through a fine sieve, pressing hard with a wooden spoon to extract as much liquid as possible. Canned coconut milk is very convenient and quite good. If a recipe calls for thick coconut milk, open the can and remove the thick milk that rises to the top. Use the contents just below the thick milk in recipes that call for light coconut milk. When the recipe calls for coconut milk, shake the can before opening.

**Coriander**, *phak chi*, Coriandrum sativum, is of the parsley family. The leaves (referred to as cilantro in the text) and stems are eaten fresh and used frequently as a garnish. The root and the seeds are ingredients in many dishes. The root is taken from the fresh plant. The seeds which are roughly spherical and range in color from off-white to brown, have a pleasant taste and fragrance. It is better to roast and grind seeds immediately before use than to buy ground coriander seeds.

**Corn Flour.** What in many parts of Asia is called corn flour we call corn starch. So for the recipes in this cook book corn flour means corn starch.

**Cucumber, Asian**, *taeng kwa*, has short fruits about 8 cm long which are crispiest while still green and white, before yellowing. A larger type, *taeng ran* is also eaten.

**Cumin**, *yi ra*, Cuminium cyminum, has elongated yellow-brown seeds about 5 mm in length. They should be dry roasted before use to heighten their fragrance.

**Curry Powder,** *phong ka-ri*, is a prepared mixture of spices such as turmeric, coriander seeds, ginger, cloves, cinnamon, mustard, cardamom, cumin, chili and salt. Each brand has its own character depending on the ingredients used.

**Ear Fungus**, *het hu nu*, is a dark grayish brown fungus that has a delightful crunchy texture. Soak in hot water for about 15 minutes and rinse well before use.

**Eggplant**, *ma kheua*, Solanum spp. In Thai cooking there are several types of eggplant aside from the more common long, thin lavender Chinese eggplant or the smaller nearly black Japanese eggplant. *Ma kheua yao* tastes very similar to Chinese and Japanese eggplant except they are green. These are served grilled, broiled or in curries. *Ma kheua phung, Solanum torvum*, grow in clusters and look like large peas. These miniature eggplants are slightly bitter but they nicely offset the rich taste of the curries in which they are used. *Ma kheua pro* is about the size of a ping pong ball. They can be white with a green cap, yellow-orange or purple in color. This eggplant is often eaten raw with a dipping sauce, or slightly cooked in a salads or curries.

**Fish Sauce,** *nam pla*, is a clear brown liquid derived from a brew of fish or shrimp mixed with salt. It is sold in bottles and plastic jugs as well as in earthenware jars. High quality fish sauce has a fine aroma and taste. Fish sauce is placed on the table as a condiment at nearly every meal, either as is or mixed with sliced chilies and perhaps lime juice.

**Five Spice Powder,** *phong pha-loh*, is a prepared mixture of Sichuan peppercorns, fennel, clove cinnamon and star anise.

**Galangal,** *kha, Alpinia galangal*, is a larger and lighter colored relative of ginger and has its own distinctive flavor.

**Ginger,** *khing, Zingiber officinale*, grows from an underground stem, or rhizome. Mature ginger stems are buff colored. Young or fresh ginger, *khing on*, is white and is eaten fresh and pickled as well as cooked.

**Gluten**, see pages 214-217

**Kaffir Lime,** *ma-krut, Citrus hystrix*, has green fruits with wrinkled skin. The rind and leaves are used in Thai cooking.

**Krachai,** *Kaempferia panduratum*, sometimes known as lesser galangal grows in bunches of slender and short yellowish brown tuberous roots and is most often used in fish dishes.

**Lemon grass,** *ta-khrai, Cymbopogon citratus*, is an aromatic green grass. The bases of the stems are used in cooking.

**Lily Buds,** *dok mai jeen, Hemerocallis spp*, are the dried unopened flowers of a type of day lily. The bright yellow buds will be fresher than the dark and brittle ones, which are old. Soak in hot water for 15-20 minutes or until soft. Cut off and discard the tough ends of the dried lily.

**Lime Solution** (*calcium hydroxide*), a mixture of lime (*calcium oxide*) and water. Used in the making of some Thai desserts to prevent flour from becoming mushy. Lime is used in the making of corn tortillas. Your local Mexican food market should stock it. Does not mean lime juice and water.

**Maggi Sauce** is the brand name of a seasoning sauce that is made from water, corn gluten, soy protein and salt. It is used in many Thai recipes and should be available in most Asian markets.

**Mushrooms, Cloud Ear's**, see Ear Fungus.

**Mushrooms, Straw**, *het fang*, used in soups, salads and curries. Straw mushrooms have a sweet and nutty flavor and although they are available canned we suggest you substitute a fresh alternative such as oyster mushrooms.

**Noodles, egg,** *ba mi*, are yellow noodles made from wheat flour and eggs. Small balls of this kind of noodle are available in the market.

**Noodles, mung bean,** *wun sen*, are thread-like noodles made from mung bean flour. They are sold dried and are soaked in water before use. When cooked they become transparent. High quality noodles maintain their integrity in soup better than do cheap ones.

**Noodles, rice,** *kuai-tiao*, are flat white noodles made from rice flour. Uncut fresh noodle sheets are sold in the market. They are also sold in three widths: wide, *sen yai* (2-3 cm), narrow, *sen lek* (5 mm) and thin, *sen mi* (1-2 mm). Dried noodles are soaked in water before use to soften them.

**Noodles, vermicelli,** *khanom jin*, are thin round noodles, made from either wheat or rice flour. Fresh vermicelli are sold in the form of wads that look like birds nests.

**Oyster Sauce,** *nam man hoi*, is a rich, viscous seasoning sauce made from fresh oysters, salt and spices. A wonderful and popular seasoning for seafood, meat and poultry. It is especially good over stir fried vegetables such as *kai lan*, *bok choy* and *choy sam*.

**Palm Sugar,** *nam tan pep*, was originally made from the sap of the sugar Palmyra palm, *Borassus flabellifera*, called *tan* in Thai, which has a very rough trunk and large, fan-shaped leaves. Now it is generally made from the sap of coconut palms and may be sold as coconut sugar. The sugar is a light golden brown paste with a distinctive flavor and fragrance. see page 173

**Pandan Leaf,** see page 203.

**Peppercorns,** *phrik thai, piper nigrum*, see page 178

**Pickled plum,** *buai dong*, is the preserved fruit of an oriental plum which is sometimes labeled Japanese apricot.

**Prawns, dried,** *kung haeng*, are small shrimp which have been dried in the sun. Look for the bright orange ones as they are the best. Dried shrimps should be soaked in hot water or rice wine before use. The soaking liquid can also be used.

**Radish, preserved,** sometimes called salted turnip, is available in Asian markets. It should be washed before use.

**Rice,** *khao jao*, the staple food in the central and southern parts of Thailand, is long-grained, non-glutinous rice. Uncooked grains are translucent. When cooked, the rice is white and fluffy.

**Rice, fermented,** *khao niao*, is made by fermenting cooked glutinous rice and is sold as a sweet.

**Rice, glutinous,** *khao niao*, also know as sticky rice, is the mainstay of the diet in the northern and northeastern regions of the country and is used in confections in all regions. Uncooked grains are starchy white in color.

**Rice Flour,** *paeng khao jao*, is made from non-glutinous rice.

**Rice Flour, glutinous,** *paeng khao niao*, is made from glutinous rice.

**Rice Paper,** made from a mixture of rice flour, water and salt. Rice paper needs to be softened before use. Carefully dip one or two sheets in a warm sugar-water solution and soak until soft, a minute or two. Drain on a towel before rolling. Look for white rice papers. Stay away from packages with broken pieces and yellowish papers.

**Rice wine,** brewed from glutinous rice. Use Chinese Shaoxing rice wine for the recipes in this book (A good, dry pale sherry can be substituted). Japanese rice wine, *sake*, is quite different and should not be used.

**Sago,** a starchy foodstuff derived from the soft interior of the trunk of various palms and cycads, used in making puddings.

**Shallots,** *hom lek or hom daeng, Allium ascalonicum*, is the zesty small red onion favored in Thai cooking.

**Shrimp Paste,** *ka-pi*, is shrimp which are salted, fermented for a time, allowed to dry in the sun then ground and worked with the addition of moisture into a fine-textured paste, which is fragrant and slightly salty. A little bit goes a long way for the Western palate.

**Sichuan Pepper,** *Zanthoxylum simulans*, also known as Chinese pepper, (except in China where it is called flower peppers) are a reddish-brown color with a pungent aroma and astringent flavor.

**Soy Sauce,** *si iu*, used in these recipes is the Chinese rather than the Japanese type. Soy sauce is prepared from a mixture of soybeans, flour and water, which is fermented and aged. The three most commonly used soy sauces are light soy sauce (*si iu khao*), dark soy sauce (*si iu dam*) and mushroom soy sauce. Light soy sauce can be substituted as a vegetarian alternative to fish sauce. Dark soy sauce is aged longer than light soy sauce and is slightly thicker, sweeter and stronger although light soy sauce is usually saltier. The dark soy sauce is preferable for dipping while the light soy sauce is most often used in cooking. Mushroom soy sauce is infused with straw mushrooms and imparts a delicious flavor.

**Star Anise,** *poi kak bua, Illicium verum*, a small, dried, dark brown, star-shaped spice with many pods. Star anise has a pungent licorice flavor. When a recipe calls for one whole star anise, it means eight individual pods. Buy star anise whole and not broken in pieces. It is most often used in braised dishes to which it imparts a rich taste and delightful fragrance.

**Sugar,** *nam tan sai*, is granulated cane sugar. Colors range from white to reddish and textures from fine to coarse. Some people find the reddish sugar tastier than the more highly refined white.

**Tamarind,** *ma-kham, Tamarindus indica*, is a tree which bears tan pods inside of which are bean-like hard brown seeds surrounded by sticky flesh. The tan pod shell can be easily removed. Ripe tamarind, ma-kham piak, is the flesh, seeds, and veins, of several fruits pressed together in the hand to form a wad. The immature fruit, the young leaves and the flowers are also used, all to give a sour taste.

**Tamarind Juice,** *nam som ma-kham*, is obtained by mixing some of the ripe fruit with water and squeezing out the juice.

**Tapioca Pellets,** *sa-khu met lek*, are tiny balls (about 2 mm in diameter) made from tapioca (cassava tubers), used in some sweets. They should be mixed with hot, but not scalding, water and kneaded, and allowed to stand for a time covered with a damp cloth to permit the water to penetrate to the core.

**Tapioca Flour,** *paeng man sampalang*, is made from tapioca, or cassava tubers. When this or any of other flour is used to thicken a sauce it is first mixed with a little water so it will not lump in the sauce.

**Tofu,** see bean curd.

**Turmeric,** *kha-min, Curcuma longa*, is a small ginger with brown rhizomes. Inside the flesh is a bright carrot orange. Also used as a coloring agent.

**Water Chestnut,** *haeo*, is the tuber of certain kinds of sedges. The skin is dark and the crunchy meat inside is off-white.

**Wax Gourd,** *fak khiao*, Benincasa hispida, also called white gourd or Chinese preserving melon, is oblong and light green to white. The ends are rounded and the flesh is solid and white.

**Won Ton Skins**, it is no longer necessary to make these by hand. Very good commercially made wrappers are available at most markets. Buy the very thin ones if possible. They freeze very well, so you can use what you need and wrap the unused wrappers well before freezing.